Your 3-D Glasses

Cut the top off the plastic storage bag and try your glasses on for size. Try folding at the outside crease if you need a tighter fit.

With the glasses on, the pictures in this book will expand into full depth . . .

. . . like this! As your eyes adjust you will become more aware of the depth.

© 1981 DC Comics

Save your glasses. Store them in the plastic pocket. They can be used to watch 3-D television too.

On My Own Two Feet

Helping Your Baby with Hypotonia Learn to Walk

Elisabeth and Patrick Callahan

Copyright © 2009 Baby Walk LLC

The stories, information, activities and games discussed in this book are intended only for your information, education and reference. This book does not constitute medical, healthcare, legal or financial advice and you should not consider it as such. We do not intend, and you should not consider, this book to substitute for consulting a pediatrician or a physical therapist to diagnose and assist with your baby's particular needs. As a recurring theme throughout the book, we frequently suggest that you seek the advice of your pediatrician or other healthcare provider with any questions you may have concerning an actual or possible medical condition or the appropriateness of any physical activity we discuss.

We would like to give special thanks to those family and friends who helped us get through this project:

Zsa-Zsa, Nana, Kyle, Karim

and to our editors –

Karen, Katy, Erin, Jan & Robin.

We must also give a special thank you to those who helped Lynn get on her feet.

Ms. Julie, Dr. Elizabeth, Dr. Joanne, Marc, and "Babies Can't Wait".

Table of Contents

What this Book is About

First, let us thank you for purchasing this book. We wish the best of luck to you and your baby on your road to walking together. It may not be a short or easy road, but you can still try to make it fun with your baby.

We created this book (along with our companion web site, www.helpyourbabywalk.com) for parents with a baby who is, or may be, delayed in the development of the ability to walk. There are many reasons why your baby may be delayed in walking, and we will mention some of those reasons throughout the book. Our baby, Lynn, was delayed in her walking due to a condition called *hypotonia*, but we hope the information and guidance in this book will be useful to parents and babies in a broad range of circumstances.

Since each baby's physical development and health condition is different, we cannot predict or guarantee how your baby will respond to the games, activities and methods described in this book, but we truly hope that your baby enjoys and benefits from the activities as much as Lynn. We also hope that sharing our story will provide comfort and guidance to those parents who feel isolated by, or unprepared for, the challenges they face with their baby's development. Finally, we believe the results of our research on government resources and particular toys and products will save most parents considerable time and money as they navigate through the various decisions to be made regarding their baby's care, treatment and development.

Ultimately, parents must use their own judgment to determine what action is best for their baby. In all cases, a parent's judgment should direct them first to a pediatrician and then to other pediatric specialists as recommended by the pediatrician. But we also believe a parent cannot simply turn over all responsibility for their child's health and development to a pediatrician. Parents must continually advocate for their baby and make certain that they, as parents, are working with their pediatricians and other specialists to do everything reasonably necessary to promote their baby's development. In all cases, you should consult and listen closely to your pediatrician and share any concerns you have about your baby's development or other information you think is relevant. In some cases, you may need to seek a second opinion from another pediatrician or contact a particular pediatric specialist to help rule out worse case scenarios. In each decision you make, you must ask yourself the same question: "Is this action (or inaction) in the best interest of my baby's health and development?"

Because this book is directed at parents, (not necessarily doctors or physical therapists,) we have included a glossary at the back of the book with certain terms and phrases that may not be part of your daily vocabulary. Elisabeth has a medical background and could easily understand the doctors and physical therapists when they used technical terms, but Patrick just nodded and tried to make mental notes to remind Elisabeth to translate the medical jargon in the minivan on the way home. We have tried to make this book, and particularly our description of the activities, as easy to understand as possible. But if there is a term or phrase that you do not understand, you should know that all *italicized* words are defined in the glossary.

The American Academy of Pediatrics (AAP) identifies certain time ranges for the "normal" or "average" development of certain *gross motor skills* in babies including rolling over (6 months), sitting up (6 – 7 months) and walking (11 - 15 months). Just as some babies take their first steps at 8 months, others might not walk until 18 months or later despite a perfectly clean bill of health from the *pediatrician*. In other cases, a child's walking may be delayed for a particular health reason (as in Lynn's case). For parents with a baby whose physical development is delayed or on the latter end of these "normal" ranges, it can be very worrisome regardless of whether your baby has a diagnosed medical condition causing the delay.

As we describe in more detail later, Lynn was a late bloomer in all her *gross motor skill* development, and we would be lying if we said the walking delay was not difficult for us. We felt very self-conscious and, at times, defensive about Lynn's delayed walking, particularly after other babies Lynn's age had been walking for months while Lynn still showed no signs of solo-standing or walking. We wanted to know what we could do ourselves on a daily basis to help Lynn learn to walk.

Please note: *This book is not meant to rush your baby*.

Your baby will walk when developmentally ready and no sooner. However, being patient with your baby's development does not mean you must be passive. Parents can and must take an active role in their baby's development – physically, mentally, and emotionally. Whether your baby just needs some extra time to develop certain *gross motor skills* or needs special attention to overcome certain physical challenges that are hindering development, you must be attentive, encouraging and persistent to help your baby make progress. We encourage you to become knowledgeable about the warning signs associated with developmental delays, attentive to your baby's progress, and forthcoming with your baby's *pediatrician* if you are concerned about your baby's development at any stage.

Later in this book, we discuss developmental timelines and warning signs at various ages that may indicate a developmental delay, but there is no substitute for a parent's intuition about their child. Early warning signs of a developmental delay can help you focus on certain aspects of your baby's development and be more proactive if a walking delay becomes more likely, but warning signs are not always a perfect predictor that your baby will have a walking delay. Even if your baby has not missed a developmental milestone, if you are concerned about your baby's development, make sure to discuss your concerns with your baby's *pediatrician*. If special attention, such as *physical therapy*, is appropriate to address your baby's development, then it is usually best to begin as early as reasonably necessary to start making progress.

Even after progress is made and your baby learns to walk, the work is not over! As many others will tell you, it does not get any easier after your baby begins walking!

Sometimes the *physical therapy* or other special attention to assist your baby's walking development may need to continue after your baby begins walking. Whether this extra work is needed or not, walking is a truly significant and life changing developmental milestone for a baby, and you and your baby can be proud and excited for achieving it.

As we worked with Lynn to overcome her own challenges, we were lucky to have a very knowledgeable and proactive *pediatrician* to help guide us through the process. However, we were very disappointed by the lack of other resources available to parents who want to help their baby's basic walking development. We found some books and videos that were clearly directed at the medical community, some of which were fairly outdated (we knew this from both the copyrights and the unmistakable fashion and hairstyles). We found some slightly relevant materials online buried in web sites and blogs. We found some chat rooms that were helpful in providing a sense that there is a community of parents experiencing similar difficulties, but the focus of these chat rooms and message boards was not specifically dedicated to helping babies to walk. All we really wanted to know is what we could do to help Lynn's walking development on the days she did not see the doctor or the physical therapist.

Ultimately, we had to teach ourselves what we could do for Lynn from piecing together information we found in various literature, web sites, and blogs and advice we received from doctors, physical therapists, family, and friends. It has truly been a learning experience for us, but we would have preferred to have some cliff notes; hence, our motivation for writing this book for you.

As noted above, every baby is different, so your experiences will most likely not mirror ours exactly. However, your experience should likely overlap with ours at various points on the road to walking, so we hope you will find most of the stories, information, products, activities and suggestions to be helpful and fun for you and your baby.

Because every baby is different, you should remember your goal is very simple: <u>You want your baby to be able to walk</u>. This is not a relative goal. You should not be concerned with your baby catching up with the other babies in the neighborhood or play-group, the ages when your other babies walked, or getting back on track with "normal" development timetables. The objective is to offer encouragement and assistance until your baby is able to walk. Whether your baby's walking is delayed because of a condition requiring special attention or your child is simply taking more time than others, there are dozens of things you can do yourself to help your baby walk.

Who We Are

Our names are Elisabeth and Patrick. We were married in 2003, and live in Georgia. We have one child, a daughter named Lynn, who was born in 2007 and is the greatest source of joy in our lives. We absolutely could not imagine being happier, or more in love, with our baby. That is not to say that Lynn is perfect or that all our experiences with her have been a piece of cake.

Lynn was in full blown colic mode for her first 4 months. For those of you who have experienced colic, you know how difficult it can be. For the rest of you, we hope you always remain blissfully ignorant.

After the colic phase was over, life with a new baby really seemed to fall into place. Lynn's personality started to take shape and her constant smile and regular laughing became both addictive and contagious. She started learning words, playing games and developing little idiosyncrasies that just melted our hearts. She was the first grandchild for our respective parents, who all live nearby, so Lynn has had no shortage of attention and spoiling.

Around 6 months, however, our *pediatrician* noted that some of Lynn's physical traits provided some cause for concern. After being on pace in some of her early check-ups, Lynn started to lag behind in the development of certain *gross motor skills*. She was a little behind pace in rolling over and a little more behind in sitting up. The pediatrician first mentioned "*low muscle tone / hypotonia*" at the 6 month check-up and she increased her attention to Lynn's muscle tone at each subsequent appointment. The pediatrician told us there are varying degrees of *hypotonia*, but it often presents in combination with one or more other diseases or conditions. Elisabeth, a former nurse at Emory Hospital and the Emory Clinic in Atlanta, started reviewing her old text books and researching *hypotonia*, and the results of her research were not very encouraging. The other diseases and conditions of which *hypotonia* can be a symptom include genetic, neurological or muscular disorders like *Cerebral Palsy*, *Multiple Sclerosis*, and *Downs Syndrome*.

We monitored Lynn's physical development closely after her 6 month check-up, and when Lynn was still showing signs of developmental delays at her 12-month check-up, the *pediatrician* referred us to a *neurologist* to rule out certain brain-related muscle issues. The *pediatrician* also suggested that Lynn see a pediatric *physical therapist* to help Lynn develop her strength, stamina, balance, coordination, and muscle control (we refer to these general attributes collectively as "*walking skills*").

Even though we knew Lynn was a little behind schedule with walking and we had researched the possible reasons for her delay, when the pediatrician actually referred us to a *neurologist* and a *physical therapist*, it was still a difficult reality for us to face. We each come from strong athletic backgrounds, with Elisabeth a former gymnast and tumbler, and Patrick a former swimmer at the collegiate level. Although we had no delusions of our baby being a future Olympian, we never really considered the possibility that our seemingly healthy baby may have a temporary or permanent physical disability.

As you may have experienced yourself, we were surprised, very concerned, and a little defensive at the news that we need to seek the help of some pediatric specialists. We were simultaneously asking ourselves, "Is there something wrong with our baby?" and assuring ourselves and everyone else "There is <u>nothing wrong</u> with our baby."

We wondered if we had done something wrong that contributed to Lynn's delay, or perhaps we had failed to do something that we were supposed to do for Lynn (something that perhaps all the other parents were doing for their children). We fought these feelings of guilt and disappointment in ourselves but, luckily, not for too long.

We were also apprehensive to tell family and friends about the possibilities of Lynn's developmental delays. We felt confident that friends and family would be supportive and encouraging; however, we also understood that it can be difficult for someone with no experience with this type of circumstance to sympathize or fully understand our situation. We wondered if acknowledging Lynn's developmental delay would make our friends and family feel awkward or helpless.

Patrick can recall a conversation with a business associate when Lynn was about 18 months that went something like this:

Tom: Hey Patrick, how's Lynn. She's about 2 now isn't she?
Patrick: Actually, she's just 18 months.
Tom: That's great. I guess she's walking and talking. Potty training yet?
Patrick: Well, actually, she's a little behind in the walking department. But we got her fitted for some little orthotics last Friday that should help her with the walking.
Tom: (Blank stare from Tom) Oh, my gosh. I'm so sorry. I don't know what to say. How are you and Elisabeth doing with it?
Patrick: Don't worry about it, Tom. She's cute as can be, and we have her in physical therapy. Everything is going to be OK.

For some people who have not personally dealt with these types of challenges, this news can sound like the end of the world. When Patrick spoke with Tom, Tom's response had a tone of such condolence that it was as if Lynn had passed away. For friends or acquaintances like Tom who do not see you or your family on a regular basis, news like this can come as a real shock. For them, finding an appropriate response can be very difficult. It is important to be patient and confident when sharing your news with others, and you should let people know there is no need for pity.

As parents it takes time to adjust and come to terms with the reality of your baby's circumstances. It took us a while to learn this lesson as we were coming to terms with the challenges facing Lynn. When we finally began Lynn's physical therapy, we were excited and a little anxious to see how Lynn would progress. Would we notice results right away? We hoped so, despite our best efforts not to get our hopes unreasonably high. We thought maybe Lynn might only need a few physical therapy visits (or maybe just a month or two), and then things would click, and we could just move forward and put this difficult phase behind us. We were anxious, almost restless, for a quick fix. In a world where rapid results and instant gratification have become a common expectation in many parts of daily life, it just seemed like there should be an easy answer to this issue.

Of course, these attitudes were the naïve wishes of new parents to a first child. Maybe a similar naivety exists in experienced parents who never had to deal with developmental delays with previous babies. With the first baby, everything is new and there is no frame of reference. With expectations from previous baby experiences for comparison, developmental delays may be even more noticeable and potentially more upsetting. In either case, the expectations create the anxiety...

Whether you are a new parent expecting (or at least hoping) that everything with your baby will be perfect (or at least "normal") or you are an experienced parent whose expectations and hopes have been set by one or more previous children, your expectations may be setting you up for anxiety and disappointment. After all, disappointment is usually a result of unrealized expectations about a particular outcome. We are not recommending that you should set your expectations for the absolute worst outcome to reduce the chance of disappointment. We are also not advising against setting lofty goals.

We are suggesting a perspective change.

In order for most goals to be effective, they must have a deadline or a timeline for motivating action and gauging progress toward a final objective. But for the goal of helping your baby walk, you have to drop the deadlines. You must forget all the "normal" developmental timetables and eliminate any sense of urgency in this goal. Do not place on yourself or your baby the pressure that accompanies such deadlines. This is a not a race and there is no prize for first place. Even if there was a prize, that would have been awarded months ago anyway to that baby down the street who walked at 8 months, so there is no point in thinking about it now, right?

This suggestion may sound obvious, and the concept of setting deadlines for our baby sounds silly when you say it out loud, but we all do it either intentionally or not, consciously or subconsciously. We may say to our spouse or think to ourselves in late August, 'I'm sure the baby will be walking by Halloween'. Then when that deadline is missed, we adjust our deadline to Thanksgiving or New Years to soften the disappointment.

Just focus on the goal (WALKING) and drop the deadlines.

This was extremely difficult for us. We both have 'type A' personalities and are very goal and deadline oriented. Patrick is in a service business where he keeps track of his time in 6 minute increments, so deadlines, efficiency and productivity is a way of life for him. He has to check that tendency at the door every time he comes home from work to play with Lynn. It is not about immediate results. It's about eventual results.

Patience, Patience, Patience… It is much easier said than done. As you'll read in the next chapter, the process you may have to go through with doctors, specialists, therapists and others can take anywhere from a couple months to a year or more. But as the old cliché goes, you just have to take it one step at a time.

Our Path to Walking

"Is this really what it's like being a parent? I have a new found respect for my parents…"

We found ourselves revolving around this idea for many months as we dove deeper into the process of helping Lynn learn to walk. Even prior to Lynn's walking issues, we had to see various other pediatric specialists to rule out a range of other possible health issues. We saw a *gastroenterologist, cardiologist, pediatric surgeon, orthopedist, pulmonologist* and a *dermatologist*. Fortunately for us and Lynn, all these possible issues turned out to be fine, but it still left us feeling like we would never get a week off from seeing some kind of doctor for Lynn.

In our adult lives we have taken our own health for granted. We are fortunate to rarely get sick or need to see a doctor, so when doctor visits became a regular occurrence for Lynn it was a real adjustment. By the time Lynn was 12 months, we had become so accustomed to regular doctor visits that we had a running joke about what new specialist we would be referred to after Lynn's next check up.

Lynn's doctor visits and medical experiences, discussed below, relating directly or indirectly to her walking are not necessarily an exact preview of what your baby will experience, but it represents one possible track. Whether your baby's condition and abilities are similar to Lynn's or substantially different, we hope you will find enough in common with our experiences that our story can prepare you for some of the challenges ahead and provide some hope that there is a light at the end of the tunnel.

Before we go into detail about the steps we took and the doctors and specialists we saw along the way to helping Lynn walk, it makes sense to discuss the reason for Lynn's walking delay. If your baby has not been diagnosed by your *pediatrician* but the discussion below sounds familiar, talk with your *pediatrician* about *hypotonia*. If your baby has been diagnosed with a condition other than *hypotonia*, our general discussion of *hypotonia* may be useful to gauge what parts of our experiences with Lynn may still apply to your situation. If you are uncertain what aspects of our experiences with Lynn are relevant to your situation, consult your *pediatrician*.

Why Lynn Was Delayed in Walking – What is Hypotonia?

Lynn's *pediatrician* and other specialists agreed that the reason for Lynn's delayed walking was a muscle condition called *hypotonia*. Each year, thousands of people are diagnosed with some form of *hypotonia* which causes decreased or low muscle tone. A person's muscles continuously receive information and instructions from the brain, whether to relax or to contract and build up tension. The precise combination of contraction in some muscles and relaxation in others enables a person to keep in a certain position or posture. If this balance of muscle contraction and relaxation is altered, then a person is able to change positions or move parts of our body. In general, the muscles of a baby with *hypotonia* are i) slower to respond to the contraction messages received from the brain, and ii) not able to maintain the intensity of the contraction for an extended time period. Together, these issues can cause difficulty or delay in sitting independently, crawling or even standing and walking which is why *hypotonia* is usually diagnosed early in life when a baby is not reaching developmental milestones when expected. As parents, you should bring up any developmental delays with your baby's *pediatrician*. (*Hypotonia*, n.d.).

In diagnosing Lynn with *hypotonia*, our *pediatrician* and other specialists emphasized that *hypotonia* is usually a symptom that accompanies another more serious disease or medical condition such as a neurological, muscle or a genetic disorder, but sometimes doctors are unable to explain why an infant has *hypotonia*; this is referred to as *benign congenital hypotonia* (*Hypotonia*, n.d.). After months of doctor visits and all the tests described below, our *pediatrician, neurologist* and *physical therapist* tend to agree that Lynn's condition is *benign congenital hypotonia.*

If a baby has *hypotonia*, it does not necessarily mean the baby's muscles are weak, although sometimes *hypotonia* and muscle weakness occur together. Infants with *hypotonia* are often very flexible and loose; traits we have always noticed in Lynn. From a sitting position, Lynn was able to pull her legs through a middle split and end up on her belly. Even after she could walk, we would find Lynn sleeping in her crib "folded in half" as if she sat up in her sleep and then just lay down with her stomach flat on the mattress between her legs. Her body and muscles have also always felt very soft to the touch although she appears to be long and relatively lean. Due to the muscle looseness and decreased muscle tone, babies with *hypotonia* are often delayed in their gross and fine motor development, and they typically do not reach developmental milestones, such as sitting up and walking, until long after their peers (*Hypotonia*, n.d.).

Most babies with *hypotonia* will continue to have some degree of *hypotonia* throughout life. With treatment, most babies can improve muscle strength, coordination and balance. Babies with mild cases may not need ongoing treatment and may eventually catch up with their peers, but they may never be the fastest or most coordinated on the playground. It is important for parents to remember to have patience and know they are doing everything possible to help their baby (*Hypotonia*, n.d.).

Hypotonia can usually be classified as central *hypotonia* or peripheral *hypotonia*. Central *hypotonia* originates from the central nervous system, while peripheral *hypotonia* is caused by problems in the skeletal muscle or peripheral nerves. Central and peripheral *hypotonia* can occur together in some diseases or conditions. The list below shows a few of the diseases and conditions that can cause *hypotonia (Diseases and Conditions*, n.d.).

- *Congenital hypothyroidism*
- *Down syndrome*
- *Marfan syndrome*
- *Muscular dystrophy*
- *Myasthenia gravis*

- *Prader-Willi syndrome*
- *Spinal muscular atrophy type 1 (Werdnig-Hoffman)*
- *Tay-Sachs disease*
- *Metabolism disorders*
- *Structural changes of the spinal cord*

For more comprehensive lists and discussion of diseases and conditions that can cause *hypotonia*, please visit our web site's parent resources page.

There can be many other reasons, aside from *hypotonia*, to explain why your baby is delayed in walking. Keep in mind that your baby may not even have a condition to diagnose. Some babies are late walkers but do not have any diseases or conditions to diagnose. We have heard many stories from parents who said their youngest baby took the longest to walk because the parents always kept the baby in the infant carrier or picked the baby up while the family was doing things with their older children. Other parents say their first baby walked late because everyone wanted to hold the new baby all the time. Of course, if you have a concern about your baby's health, you should check with your baby's *pediatrician* for a diagnosis based on your baby's individual history and examination (*Hypotonia*, n.d.).

Pediatrician

As we have said before and will say again, if you believe your child has any health issues including possible developmental delays, you should consult your *pediatrician* for a diagnosis and recommendations on how best to address your baby's health or developmental issue. During your baby's first year, your *pediatrician* will likely want to see your baby for at least 6 scheduled check-ups. The purpose of the frequency of these visits is to improve the chances of identifying health or developmental issues as early as possible. In some cases, the *pediatrician* will refer your baby to other specialists for further evaluation. The pediatrician is the second line of defense for your baby's health and development. Parents and caretakers are the first line of defense and bear primary responsibility for a baby's wellbeing.

In our case, Lynn's *pediatrician* was extremely proactive and attentive to Lynn's circumstances and particular needs. She identified Lynn's *hypotonia* very early and was always careful to consider how the *hypotonia* might affect Lynn's development or other common health issues. When it was clear at Lynn's 12-month check-up that Lynn would be a late walker, the pediatrician referred us to a *neurologist* to check for, and hopefully rule out, certain muscle, neurological or genetic disorders like those listed in the previous section. Although we expected that Lynn would probably need to see a specialist for *hypotonia*, it was still upsetting when the *pediatrician* actually referred us to a *neurologist* because it forced us to face the possibility that Lynn had a more serious disease or condition. We set up the first appointment available which was a full 6 weeks away!!!

Our *pediatrician* also suggested physical therapy to help Lynn develop walking skills. Before we took the plunge with physical therapy, we decided to wait and get the *neurologist*'s opinion. In retrospect, part of our decision to wait on the physical therapy was the result of simple parental denial that our baby needed therapy. We were trying to convince ourselves, "She's just a little behind, that's all". Candidly, our decision to wait before beginning physical therapy also had to do with the anticipated expense of therapy which would largely not be covered by our medical insurance. (We provide a more detailed discussion of the medical expenses, insurance coverage and other financial resources that may be available to you in Chapter 5.) If we had to do it over again, we would have initiated physical therapy when our *pediatrician* first recommended it. As we have progressed through all our experiences with Lynn, we have moved further away from the "wait and see" philosophy in favor of a more proactive attitude.

Neurologist

By that time we saw the *neurologist*, we were getting anxious. Lynn's main way of getting around (at 13 ½ months) was still rolling and "army crawling" on her forearms. After some very playful interaction with Lynn, the *neurologist* said she was not very concerned about the severity of Lynn's condition. The *neurologist* noted that Lynn had very good posture when sitting, had excellent fine motor skills, and had an energetic and interactive personality. The *neurologist* ordered some blood work to do some preliminary screening, and told us to schedule a follow up visit for 3 months to reevaluate Lynn. If Lynn was still noticeably behind at that point, we could do further testing and diagnosis. Then, the *neurologist* reiterated our *pediatrician*'s physical therapy recommendation and said Lynn could benefit greatly from some exercises to develop her strength and muscle control.

Blood Work

Both the *pediatrician* and *neurologist* ordered multiple blood tests to look for causes of Lynn's *hypotonia*. Each time a test was ordered we had to go to the local children's hospital to have Lynn's blood drawn. She did well the first couple times, but after she learned to recognize the lab, she knew she was going to get poked with a needle and became less cooperative for subsequent appointments. Luckily, the technician drawing the blood could apply a numbing cream prior to the blood draw to help make the process easier. The hardest part was keeping Lynn entertained while we waited.

Initially our *pediatrician* ordered a *karyotype* to look for any abnormalities with Lynn's chromosomes that would indicate a genetic cause of the *hypotonia*.

The *neurologist* ordered further blood and urine tests to analyze the levels of certain enzymes and other substances in Lynn's body that may help identify or rule out one or more diseases or conditions causing Lynn's *hypotonia*. These tests looked for substances including muscle enzymes, amino acids, lactic acid, pyruvic acid, carnitine, and urine organic acids. Since we are not physicians, the particular diagnostic objectives of these tests are beyond our ability to explain in detail. However, as it was generally explained to us, these tests were intended to show whether i) Lynn's muscles show signs of damage that would suggest a possible neuromuscular disease, or ii) Lynn's body was having difficulty converting food to energy that would suggest a possible metabolic disease. We felt fortunate that all of these tests came back normal.

Physical Therapy

Our next step was to identify a *physical therapist,* since neither the *pediatrician* nor *neurologist* gave us any specific names. As we discuss in more detail later, we ended up connecting with a *physical therapist* through Georgia's statewide Early Intervention Program for babies with physical disabilities, "***Babies Can't Wait***".

It took a few weeks to get all the paperwork and scheduling in order, so Lynn started working with a pediatric *physical therapist* when she was almost 14 ½ months. Lynn enjoyed the 1-hour visits every two weeks. The *physical therapist* had a great way of making therapy visits more like playing and less like work (a concept we have tried to incorporate throughout the activities we suggest later). Our *physical therapist* would loan toys and devices to us for Lynn to use for weeks at a time. One device she loaned us was a baby "walker" similar to the ones you see elderly using to assist them to walk. The walker came up to Lynn's waist (about 15 inches off the ground) so Lynn could stand and hold horizontal side bars around her waist level (see picture on page 172). The walker had 4 wheels that could either be locked into a straight position for stability or unlocked to allow swiveling and turning. The *physical therapist* modified the walker so it supported Lynn from behind so Lynn was able to walk with the walker behind her and nothing in front of her. This seemed to give Lynn a sense of independently walking. Lynn loved it!!! It was like her own little prescription push toy, and it was great for building confidence and developing some of the *muscle memory* needed to know how to put one foot in front of the other among all the other subtle details that go into walking. Although this was one of the most useful gadgets in Lynn's walking development, it is something your *physical therapist* would have to recommend and tailor to the particular needs of your baby.

After a couple months of noticeable but slow progress, Lynn still was not walking, and it was clear she needed more help. We agreed with the *physical therapist*'s suggestion to increase to weekly therapy sessions, and our *physical therapist* recommended *Dynamic Ankle and Foot Orthosis (DAFOs)* for Lynn. *DAFOs* are hard plastic corrective devices that mold to the shape of her feet and lower legs, encourage proper joint alignment and give her extra stability and support when bearing weight on her legs. Since *DAFOs* are specially casted and fitted to your baby, they require a prescription from a doctor.

A follow-up visit to the *neurologist* at about 17 months confirmed some improvement, but Lynn still was not taking steps or standing on her own. She was pulling up and walking while holding on to furniture for support at this point. The *neurologist* prescribed the *DAFOs* and ordered some precautionary blood work to rule out muscle wasting diseases and an *MRI* of Lynn's brain to rule out structural problems in the brain that could cause the *hypotonia*.

MRI

The *MRI* was not a fun experience for Lynn or us. Some may be asking, 'How do you keep a baby still long enough to do an MRI?' The answer is simple: *sedatives*. Unfortunately, administering sedatives is not an easy process itself. It required Lynn to get an *IV* so the sedative could be introduced into her system. Now you may be asking, 'How do you keep a baby still long enough to start an *IV*?' The answer the nurses gave to this question was also simple to explain but hard to actually perform. Patrick and Elisabeth had to hold Lynn and restrain her arms and legs from flailing while the nurses tried repeatedly to start an *IV* in Lynn's chubby little arm and wrist. After 3 nurses made several attempts, Lynn finally had her *IV*.

The *MRI* was scheduled for mid-morning. Lynn was not supposed to eat or drink for 12 hours before she received the sedatives, so we got her right out of bed and took her to the hospital without breakfast or even her morning milk. We felt bad about it, and Lynn did not appreciate it either, but we had to follow the doctor's orders. Lynn was in a strange place, and we think she could sense that she was not going to like it. It was emotionally difficult for us to see Lynn in the hospital with a little gown and an *IV* in her arm and to know the types of conditions we were hoping the *MRI* would rule out. The most upsetting part was actually seeing Lynn pass out in our arms when the doctors put the sedative into her *IV* on the *MRI* table. Watching Lynn's open eyes roll back in her head, her jaw drop open, and her body go limp made us both cry. Then we had a 30 minute wait (which of course seemed much longer) until Lynn was returned to us groggy and unable to hold up her head. When we first picked her up after the *MRI*, it was like holding a 23 pound newborn. We had to be very careful to support her head until she was no longer groggy. Luckily, the results of the *MRI* were clear.

The doctors, nurses, and staff at the hospital were great; however, that did not keep the experience from being upsetting. Although we had seen many doctors before with Lynn and we were thinking positively that this was just a precautionary measure to rule out certain worst case scenarios, there was something about the gravity of this situation that really forced us to face all the fears and emotions associated with more serious health risks to our baby. Some who read this may breathe a sigh of relief that they have not had to go through this experience. Others may laugh and say, "An MRI is easy compared to what we've been through!!"

It is worth mentioning at this point that just as the experiences of our babies may differ, parents also will react differently even when faced with circumstances similar to those we are describing. It is important to fully process your reactions and emotions and to share them with your spouse, or other important person in your life. It is especially important for spouses to verbalize and share how they feel about their baby's health. When you are juggling emotions of love for your baby, disappointment at the circumstances, concern for the future, and hope that everything will be okay, it can be difficult to know exactly how you feel. Don't worry. That's natural. We adjusted to our circumstances over time, but it was extremely helpful to have family, friends and one another to lean on.

Orthotist

In the same week Lynn had the *MRI*, we met with a pediatric *orthotist* who took casts of Lynn's legs for the *DAFOs*. The casting process was a piece of cake – only about 3 minutes per leg. He assessed Lynn's walking abilities while she wore shoes and while she was barefoot. Lynn's right foot had always dragged and pointed out to the right when she tried to walk, either with the assistance of a walker or while holding our hands. The *orthotist* noticed that Lynn's right foot was also collapsing around her arches when she put her weight on it. The *DAFOs* would be helpful with both these issues. A few weeks later, we went back to the *orthotist*, and Lynn got her *DAFOs*. They are made from hard molded plastic and extended well beyond Lynn's toes at first. The *orthotist* trimmed back the plastic in certain places and smoothed the edges so that it would not interfere too much with Lynn's toe movement or ankles.

It was difficult for us to find shoes that fit well while Lynn was wearing the *DAFOs*, and we had to purchase several pairs to find one that worked. The *orthotist* told us the cheaper, the better. After all, the *DAFOs* would be providing all the support. The *physical therapist* told us to have Lynn wear the *DAFOs* for a half hour each day at first, but she said Lynn should work up to wearing them all day long to maximize the benefits.

We had our *physical therapist* look at the orthotics to make sure they fit correctly and were doing what she wanted. Unfortunately, they were not. The *orthotist* had trimmed too much from the toes where Lynn needed extra support and too much from the ankle where Lynn needed correction of her tendency to turn her toes out. A few weeks later, we met the *physical therapist* at the *orthotist*'s office so the *orthotist* could remake Lynn's *DAFOs* (luckily, not at an additional expense) to give Lynn the type of support that our *physical therapist* wanted. After we received the second pair, we quickly noticed an improvement in Lynn's ability to balance and position herself properly.

ENT

The week before Lynn picked up her fancy new *DAFOs*, we visited an Ear, Nose and Throat specialist (*ENT*). It was winter and Lynn had been getting colds and ear infections regularly, so our *pediatrician*, once again, directed us to a specialist to take a closer look. You may ask why this is relevant to Lynn's walking. It did not occur to us before the appointment, but the *ENT* reminded us that a person's sense of balance is largely tied to a series of tubes and fluid levels in a person's ears. If Lynn's ears are regularly infected, then that may be impacting her balance when she tries to stand or walk on her own. Due to the number of ear infections she was having the *ENT* recommended that Lynn have tubes placed in her ears to help drain fluid and have sinus surgery to remove part of her *adenoids*. Both of these procedures are fairly common for infants and toddlers.

The point of mentioning the *ENT* is that are many subtle connections in the body. There is not one specific activity you must do or one specific group of muscles that a baby must develop in order to walk. It can be difficult to see how all the pieces fit together. This is why it is critically important to consult your *pediatrician* and other specialists, if necessary, to make sure that all the pieces are working together to help your baby's development.

Geneticist

The *neurologist* recommended that Lynn see a *geneticist* to rule out certain genetic disorders. *Geneticists* specialize in diagnosing and treating diseases that are caused by a defect in a person's genes. Usually these diseases are hereditary. The process of getting an appointment was not easy because there are only a handful of *geneticists* in the United States who specialize in muscle related genetic diseases and, more specifically, mitochondrial disease. Mitochondria are the parts of our cells responsible for creating energy to fuel our bodies. Our *neurologist* told us it was important to test Lynn for mitochondrial disease because it can have very serious effects on the way her cells produce energy and the organ systems in her body. To learn more about mitochondrial disease visit www.mitoaction.org. We had to collect all of Lynn's medical records and submit them to the *geneticist* for review. After reviewing her records we got an appointment, and we were required to put down a deposit to hold our appointment. When we met the *geneticist,* he went over Lynn's medical history and recommended that Lynn have a muscle biopsy and a sample taken of her skin, blood, urine, and spinal fluid for testing. He would then look for thousands of possible genetic abnormalities and muscle related diseases. We agreed to this plan and set up the muscle biopsy with a surgeon.

Lynn underwent the muscle biopsy at an outpatient surgery center. The surgeon collected all of the samples at the same time while Lynn was sedated. The muscle biopsy involved removing a 1centimeter cube of muscle from the top of Lynn's thigh. She was in a great deal of pain and refused to walk for about a week after the surgery. We gave her prescription pain medications and tried to make her as comfortable as possible, but we could not help feeling guilty for doing this to our child. We realized it was important for us to proceed with this testing to make sure Lynn did not have a serious genetic condition that would require treatment.

After several months we received the genetic test results. We discovered that Lynn had a deletion in one of her chromosomes. The *geneticist* did not believe this was necessarily the cause of her *hypotonia,* and he recommended further testing. He also thought that he could not completely dismiss mitochondrial disease. He ran further tests on the samples he already had, and we had our blood drawn to check for this abnormality in ourselves. If either of us carried the same abnormality, it would mean that Lynn's genetic abnormality is not the cause of Lynn's *hypotonia* since neither of us has *hypotonia*.

When we followed up with the *geneticist* we found out that neither of us carried the abnormality. We also learned that Lynn had a mitochondrial "variant" meaning that she also has an abnormality in her mitochondria. The *geneticist* explained that this is something passed on genetically through the mother. He told us that Lynn's abnormalities are not causing her any severe problems and that it does not necessarily explain her *hypotonia*. He stated that over time and through advances in research we will eventually learn what all of this means. For now we will continue to follow up with the *geneticist* to monitor Lynn's progress. He suggested that we try giving her Coenzyme Q10, which is an over the counter supplement, to see if this improves her energy level and gross motor skills. It will take some time to evaluate the effectiveness of the Coenzyme Q10. During this time Lynn will be monitored by the *geneticist*.

Lynn's Baby Steps, Toddling and Walking

Each of the previous sections has described a different stage of Lynn's path to walking, and each stage played an important role in the larger picture of Lynn's development of walking skills. The most enjoyable stage, of course, was the exciting conclusion to the months of hard work and persistence when Lynn began putting the pieces together and taking some steps alone. Lynn was just over 19 months old when she let go of the coffee table for the first time and walked a couple steps toward Elisabeth. We were extremely excited, and we felt certain that Lynn had turned a corner in her development and would officially reach the walking milestone any day. However, fueled by our early excitement of Lynn's first steps, we encouraged Lynn to try taking more and more steps with each effort. As Lynn would walk towards us, we would back up just beyond her reach to try to encourage a new personal best for the number of steps taken by Lynn. After only a couple days of this game, Lynn got fed up. She learned that each walking attempt ended with a thud as she fell to the floor with her parents backing up just out of reach. In retrospect, we realize how frustrating and discouraging this must have been for Lynn.

For the next several weeks, Lynn went back to crawling, and we had a difficult time convincing her to take even a few steps. Instead of seeing Lynn's walking skills improve rapidly, our tactics backfired because we were trying to force Lynn to walk further than she was able or comfortable. Lynn's temporary "walking strike" forced us to summon a fresh dose of patience and perspective about the circumstances. We continued all our games and activities with Lynn to help develop her walking skills, and we encouraged Lynn to take steps on her own whenever appropriate. If she was cruising on furniture and we were a few feet away, we encouraged her to walk to us, but we did not assist her to stand in the middle of a room and let go of her hands so she would have to stand or walk on her own.

When Lynn was almost 20 months, she regained some of her confidence for walking, but she developed a new approach. Instead of trying to walk on her own, she would take one or both of us by the hand and lead us around the house, the yard or anywhere else she wanted to walk. She was excited by her new ability and seemed to enjoy the sense of freedom, but she still needed us for balance and, more importantly, for confidence. Lynn continued this habit for several weeks including on a family trip to Washington, DC to visit some family friends. Although we brought a stroller with us, Lynn actually preferred to walk with our assistance for most of the trip. We took many walks around the city and even went to the National Zoo for an afternoon. Lynn loved looking at the animals, and insisted on walking almost everywhere as long as one of us was holding her hand. She must have walked well over a mile that day! We knew it could not be much longer before she would be walking on her own…

The following week, she knew it too. Lynn was almost 21 months when we officially deemed her a "walker". She stood up in the family room, walked into the kitchen, turned the corner after passing the counter and walked to the trash can to throw away the wrapper from her afternoon snack bar. Then she walked back to the family room. It was a good 30 steps for Lynn. We looked at one another and erupted with cheers of congratulations for Lynn who was smiling proudly at her achievement and apparent new physical ability. For weeks after that day, Lynn continued to look a little like Frankenstein with her arms out to the side and a general appearance of instability, but this improved with time. From that day forward, Lynn walked everywhere we went.

We should note that even after Lynn reached the walking milestone, she continued to wear her *DAFOs* and we continued with physical therapy because Lynn's *hypotonia* meant she would continue to lag behind on other developmental milestones like jumping and running. Whether your baby has *hypotonia* or not, you should consult your *pediatrician* and other specialists to determine what measures, if any, are appropriate to continue after your baby begins walking.

"Normal" Developmental Timelines

There are over 4 million babies born in the United States each year (*17 Surprising Facts*, 2008). With that number of babies, there are some pretty detailed statistics about the "average" age when babies first walk and the "standard deviation" that separates early walkers, average walkers and late walkers. Despite all the available data, it still can be complicated to try and define what age is "normal" for babies to start walking or reaching other developmental milestones. There are many variables in a baby's development that cause each to develop at a unique pace whether in walking, talking, or personality traits, so there can be wide time ranges defining when it is "normal" for babies to reach these developmental milestones. Even if a baby is a late walker, though, this does not mean the baby is not "normal", and it does not necessarily mean the delayed walking is the result of a disease or condition that requires special attention or treatment.

Why, then, should we discuss normal developmental timelines if every baby's development is different? Simply put, 'it is better to be safe than sorry'.

Babies should not be forced to do something before they are developmentally ready, and this book is not intended to rush your baby. However, if your baby has a health issue that is causing, or may cause, a developmental delay, then it is best to diagnose and begin addressing that issue sooner rather than later.

A family in our neighborhood has a daughter who was diagnosed with hypotonia when she was only 2 months. The pediatrician recommended physical therapy and the parents began right away. The physical therapy was not intended to rush the baby's development but was an effort to prevent hypotonia from significantly delaying the baby's development. As a result of the early diagnosis by the pediatrician and proactive approach by the parents and physical therapist, the baby was given the best possible start to her motor development and had no significant developmental delays.

The developmental timeline outlined in this chapter provides a statistical baseline as a frame of reference from which to gauge your baby's progress through various developmental milestones. Based on our experience and from speaking with others, most parents would prefer to identify potential health issues or developmental delays as early as possible rather than taking the "wait and see" approach. For many parents, the uncertainty of not knowing if there is a health issue is worse than confirming a health issue exists. At least if a health issue exists, parents can begin acting to address it properly. Sometimes, however, developmental delays can exist without a specific diagnosable health issue or medical condition to explain it. Yet even in these cases, action still should be taken to address the developmental delay.

Early in our work with Lynn's developmental delays from *hypotonia*, we decided that if we were going to be playing with Lynn anyway, we might as well be playing in a proactive and constructive way to help Lynn develop in the right direction. This feeling of constructive assistance provided the inspiration for this book.

Below is a list of infant and toddler developmental milestones. The list also includes possible warning signs that you should report to your baby's *pediatrician* to help determine if your baby's development is delayed or at risk for a future delay. These milestones and warning signs are general guidelines, but if you have any specific concerns about your child's progress, you should talk with your *pediatrician*. Your *pediatrician* should be asking about, or looking for, these developmental milestones and warning signs at your baby's regular check-ups, but parents should always be in the best position to gauge their baby's progress. You can also refer to our web site for links to other information on developmental timelines.

One Month – By the end of the first month your baby makes jerky movements. He can move his head from side to side while on his stomach but is not able to support his head on his own. He may be able to lift his head when lying on his tummy. His hands are usually in tight fists and he can bring them towards his face.

- *Warning Sign*: If your baby seems floppy or extremely loose or if he infrequently moves his arms and legs, contact your *pediatrician* (Shelov, Hanneman, & Trubo, 1991/2004, p. [154,159]).

Three Months – By the end of the third month he should be able to raise his head and chest and support his upper body with his arms while on his stomach. He is able to hold his head steady. He should be able to kick his legs and push down on his legs when his feet are placed on a hard surface. He can open and close his hands and shake a small rattle.

- *Warning Sign*: If your baby is not able to grasp and hold objects by three months, support his head well, or push down through his legs when on a hard surface you should discuss this with your *pediatrician* (Shelov, Hanneman, & Trubo, 1991/2004, p. [180,190]).

Four Months – By the end of the fourth month, he should be able to bear weight on his legs while a parent holds him (*Milestone Charts: What,* 2006).

Six Months – By the end of the sixth month, he should be able to roll over in both directions.

- *Warning Sign*: If your baby is not able to sit with assistance, you should notify your *pediatrician* (*Milestone Charts: What,* 2006).

Seven Months – By the end of the seventh month, your baby should be able to sit up without your support.

- *Warning Sign*: If by the end of the seventh month your child seems very stiff or very floppy or if he is unable to hold up his head when pulled to a sitting position, you should notify your *pediatrician* (Shelov, Hanneman, & Trubo, 1991/2004, p. [205, 212]).

Nine Months – By the end of the ninth month, your baby should be able to pull to standing and stand while holding on to something (*Milestone Charts: What*, 2006).

Eleven months – By the end of the eleventh month, your baby should be able to stand alone for a few seconds and walk while "cruising" along furniture (*Milestone Charts: What*, 2006).

Twelve Months – At the end of the twelfth month, your baby should be able to stand unsupported for a moment, walk a few steps and sit down from standing without assistance.

- ***Warning Sign***: At twelve months, some signs of a possible developmental delay include not being able to crawl, not using both sides of his body equally while crawling, and not being able to stand with support. Notify your *pediatrician* of any of these warning signs (Shelov, Hanneman, & Trubo, 1991/2004, p. [237, 251]).

Thirteen Months – By the end of the thirteenth month, your baby should be able to bend over and pick up an object. Approximately 75% of babies have begun to walk by this age (*Milestone Charts: What*, 2006).

Fifteen Months – By the end of the fifteenth month, most babies are walking well.

- ***Warning Sign***: If your baby is not walking at fifteen months, bring this up with your doctor if you have not already (*Milestone Charts: What*, 2006).

Eighteen Months – By the end of the eighteenth month, your baby should be able to run, albeit clumsily. He should also be able to jump in place with both feet and walk up stairs with one hand held (Wong, Hockenberry-Eaton, Wilson, Winkelstein, & Schwartz, 1982/2001, p. [420-421]).

Twenty One Months – By the end of the twenty-first month, your baby should be able to walk up stairs unassisted (*Milestone Charts: What*, 2006).

Twenty Two Months – By the end of the twenty-second month, your baby should be able to kick a ball (*Milestone Charts: What*, 2006).

The 13th and 15th month descriptions listed above are the benchmarks most relevant to gauge walking development, but alerting your *pediatrician* when earlier benchmarks are missed or warning signs exist can give your baby a head start on the extra attention he may need. About 75% of babies are walking by 13 months, and if your baby still is not walking by 15 months, then you should notify your *pediatrician*. If your baby is not walking by 15 months, do not panic. There are things you can do to help. After alerting your *pediatrician*, you can begin exploring the possible reasons for your baby's walking delay. If your *pediatrician* refers you to other specialists, make sure you follow doctor's orders. However, do not feel you must stop with the specialists or feel that you must sit and wait for their instructions. Remember, parents must use their own judgment and decide what is best for their baby. The activities suggested later in this book are intended for parents who want to be proactive in helping their baby's development. Please check with you *pediatrician* first to be sure these activities are appropriate for your child.

There may be some doctors who will advise you not to worry and simply to "wait and see" until the next check-up. This may be valid advice under your particular circumstances, but do not hesitate to seek a second opinion if your parental instinct tells you something is not right or something more needs to be done.

We know a delightful little boy whose parents raised concerns with their *pediatrician* for years because their son's speech did not seem to be developing at the "normal" pace. The *pediatrician* kept advising the parents to "wait and see" until the next check-up. Finally, at the boy's 3-year check-up the parents vehemently insisted that their son be tested to see what may be causing his speech delays. Fortunately, tests for brain related disorders and autism came back negative. However, hearing tests revealed that the boy was almost entirely deaf. The parents regretted not following their instincts sooner, and they felt that the doctor's "wait and see" advice and their "patience" essentially delayed by 2 years their son's speech therapy and hearing aid use so he could begin hearing and learning to speak.

"Wait and see" is fairly common advice, and if your *pediatrician* has ruled out many of the most likely "worst case scenarios", then a "wait and see" approach might be appropriate and acceptable to you. However, if no action is taken to identify or at least rule out some of the more common conditions that could be delaying your baby's walking, then a "wait and see" approach could leave your child in a position you may regret later.

Adjusting to Your Baby's Developmental Delays and Talking with Others

As Lynn's personality developed, it overshadowed all other physical issues that Lynn was facing. Anyone who has met Lynn can tell you she is just incredible – walking or not – and we are sure you take the same pride in your baby. So when we told people that Lynn could not walk yet at 15 months, or later at 18 months, we did not want them to respond with pity. We did not want people to confuse Lynn's developmental delay with a permanent disability. We also did not want Lynn's delay or possible permanent disability to alter anyone's opinion of Lynn as a child; we did not want them to feel sorry for her or expect less from her mental or personality development.

We never felt sorry for Lynn. We maintained a positive attitude and had confidence she would walk eventually with some extra help from us, our family and the physical therapist. Even if you do not have the same full confidence in your baby's walking prospects, you are most likely not looking for others' pity either.

It is understandable, however, that when we described Lynn's circumstances to people who were not familiar with her or had no similar personal experiences, some of those people viewed Lynn's situation as a terrible setback. You may have even jumped to similarly grim conclusions when you first learned your baby was delayed and a permanent disability was a possibility. But after getting over the initial shock of a baby's circumstances, parents have time to internalize, accept and adjust to the new situation. As parents, we realized that Lynn's condition did require her to use a walker, wear orthotics and receive physical therapy, but we tried to maintain a good perspective about the larger picture. We regularly read message boards in chat rooms about babies with developmental delays who were in far worse shape than Lynn, and these stories put Lynn's condition into perspective. While this made us feel relatively fortunate, we had to remember that most of our friends, family and acquaintances did not have the benefits of the same research or perspective. After all, their children probably never needed a walker, orthotics, or physical therapy. It is unreasonable to expect others to go through the same mental and emotional adjustments in the span of a conversation, phone call or introduction that parents go through over the course of months. We found that once people hear your positive attitude towards your situation, it makes it easier for them to react with encouragement, rather than pity.

This is not to say that parents cannot have moments of doubt and discouragement, but as parents, we all must live with a general sense of hope about our child's future. This is not blind optimism. We all love our babies, and it is important to believe in their potential and appreciate all their positive attributes. Part of this attitude is for the baby's confidence and well-being, and part of this attitude is for our sanity and well-being as parents.

We derive much of our own self-confidence from other aspects of our life that we feel are successful or that fill us with pride. As a parent, it is easy to allow our pride in our baby to fuel our self-confidence just as a strong and loving marriage or a good career or enjoyable job also fill us with confidence. What if our child has a disability or is developmentally delayed? Does that disability or delay damage or reduce our self-confidence?

Hopefully not! What most parents learn is that regardless of a child's situation, we can always still see the beauty and potential in our baby. We are not ignoring the differences between our baby and others or the unique obstacles our baby faces. We are simply appreciating all the things our baby can do and acknowledging that our baby needs extra work in certain other areas. This general attitude applies even for babies without developmental delays. The sooner you and your baby learn to see beyond life's obstacles and focus on your goals and priorities, the better off you will be.

Lynn has a tremendous personality, smile, and laugh, and she has developed some very interesting idiosyncrasies. One thing we noticed early on is that Lynn actually likes to clean up after herself. She was 13 months when we first saw her wad up a used napkin in the family room and army crawl (which was not easy for her) into the kitchen, open a cabinet and beg for our help to pull herself to standing (which also was not easy for her) so that she could throw away the napkin in the trash can. She has been wiping up spills and throwing away trash ever since.

A baby that cleans up after herself? Now that we can **appreciate**!!!!

Once you adjust to this way of thinking, you learn to teach and convince others not to view your baby in comparison with other kids, but to appreciate what your baby can do rather than pitying your baby for what he cannot do.

Expenses, Insurance and Other Resources

Expenses

Raising a child is expensive, even without any complications like health issues and developmental delays. A government study published in 2007 estimated that the total cost of raising a child from birth to age 18 is $298,680 (*Expenditures on Children*, n.d.). This does not include any costs related to education or extra medical attention for special needs like developmental delays.

It is also unsettling to note that for many years the leading cause of personal bankruptcy in the United States has been medical debts related to illnesses, accidents or extensive medical needs. Even more unsettling is the fact that most of the people who are bankrupted by illness and medical bills had health insurance at the beginning of their illness. Most people filing for medical expense related bankruptcy were middle class citizens with 56% owning a home and the same percentage having attended college. Often the family's breadwinner became ill and was forced take time off from work, which led to lost income and lost health insurance benefits through the employer at a time when the family needed it most (Himmelstein, Warren, Thorne & Woolhandler, 2005). As we discuss below, there are certain options available when a person loses *group health insurance* through an employer. One option is to purchase *individual private health insurance* coverage, but this option can be relatively ineffective if *pre-existing condition* limitations prevent coverage for the very conditions for which a person or family members need insurance coverage the most!

Needless to say, when it comes to the health and well-being of our babies, all parents want to give their children the best treatment and care that money can buy. Realistically, we understand that most people have very real budget constraints. After Lynn was born, Elisabeth stopped working as a nurse so she could be home full time to care for Lynn. This left Patrick as the "sole breadwinner", and we relied on his income to pay the mortgage on our home, all our other regular expenses and the new baby expenses we were trying to get used to. We did not feel we were in financial distress or facing a bankruptcy scenario as described above, but we certainly were not comfortable with the idea of potentially open ended medical bills if there were gaps in our health insurance coverage.

The table below gives you an idea of some of the expenses we faced in connection with Lynn's medical diagnosis and treatment. Keep in mind; these are **not** our actual out-of-pocket costs but simply the raw costs of the medical services and products before factoring in the benefits of insurance coverage and other financial resources. Also keep in mind that medical costs may differ by medical provider and by geographic region and will increase from year to year. These were our expenses in 2008.

Descriptions of Services or Items	Amounts
Visits to the *Pediatrician*	$150 per visit
Visits to specialists like the *Neurologist, Orthotist* and *ENT* and related medical testing and procedures at those visits	$200 - $1,100
Lab work including blood and urine testing	$200 - $800
Diagnostic scans like *X-Rays, CT scans* and *MRI scans* – typically involves other charges like doctor, nurse, sedation and supply fees	$1000 - $4000 for scans and other charges
Therapy Visits – physical, occupational, speech, etc.	$100 - $300 per visit
Dynamic Ankle and Foot Orthosis (DAFOs)	$1800 per pair
Other toys and equipment specifically intended to aid Lynn's walking (We probably spent $500 out-of-pocket in total)	Items ranged from $2 - $100

Insurance Coverage

General Information

In 2007, about 46 million Americans under the age of 65 did not have health insurance. That was about 18% of the population in that age demographic ("National Coalition on Health," 2009). For those without health insurance, the prospect of providing access to adequate healthcare for a baby must already be overwhelming even without a developmental delay that could cause substantial additional expenses.

We are not experts on health insurance coverage, government assistance programs, or the laws associated with these topics, but we do know there are some options available to help cover some healthcare costs for people without health insurance. *Medicaid,* State *Title V* programs, and State *Early Intervention Programs* (discussed below) are a few of the main resources that the uninsured can contact to provide assistance.

Even for those who do have insurance, you still have your work cut out for you. As a general rule, health insurance falls into two very broad categories:

1. *Group health insurance* which is offered as an employment benefit by many employers to their employees, and

2. *Individual private health insurance* which can be purchased by individuals who do not have *group health insurance*.

In theory, *individual private health insurance* is available to anyone, but there are two primary catches; first, in most states you have to be able to qualify for it based on an initial health examination, and second, you have to be able to afford it. These catches help explain the statistic above about the number of uninsured in 2007. *Individual private health insurance* often comes with higher monthly premiums, higher co-pay levels, higher deductibles, less flexibility and lower benefits relative to *group health insurance*. By far the worst drawback of *individual private health insurance* is the dreaded "*pre-existing condition*". If you want *individual private health insurance*, you must first go through an extensive application process and the insurance company will ask for all your medical records as far back as you can go. If your medical history shows evidence of a particular disease or condition (anything from asthma to acid reflux) then those diseases or conditions will not even be covered by your *individual private health insurance*. Still, the risk of facing the rising cost of healthcare and medical expenses without having health insurance makes even the more expensive and limited *individual private health insurance* appear to be a very necessary expense.

Group health insurance is generally preferable to *individual private health insurance* for a number of reasons. *Group health insurance* is usually less expensive to an individual or family because employers often pay at least a portion of the insurance *premium*. According to the Kaiser Family Foundation, a California based nonprofit company focused on healthcare policy, employees with *group health insurance* paid an average *premium* of about $694 a year for health insurance coverage in 2007 with the company picking up the rest of the *premium* bill – approximately $3,785 a year (Bradford, 2008). In comparison, an individual could pay anywhere from $1,800 to over $12,000 per year in *premiums* for *individual private health insurance* depending upon a range of factors. For *group health insurance* for a family, employees paid an average *premium* of $3,281 a year with the company's share of the *premium* cost rising to an average of $8,824. Meanwhile, *individual private health insurance* for a family could easily reach *premiums* of $10,000 to $15,000 or more. *Group health insurance* is also not subject to some of the restrictions, exceptions and limitations that are common with almost all *individual private health insurance* such as non-coverage for *"pre-existing conditions"*. *Group health insurance* usually comes with other ancillary products and services like *Flexible Spending Accounts* which allow a person to set aside money from each paycheck, before taxes, into an account that can be used for family medical expenses. Smart use of a *Flexible Spending Account* can help a person save a little on income taxes if big medical expenses are on the horizon or if a person's annual insurance deductible is likely to be spent in full. Just be careful and pay attention to the "use-it-or-lose-it" rules about contributions to the account.

Thanks to the Consolidated Omnibus Budget Reconciliation Act of 1985 (referred to as *"COBRA"*), *group health insurance* does not necessarily have to stop just because you lose your job. *COBRA* is a federal law that requires certain employers with at least 20 employees to provide departing employees (whether the employee quits or is fired or laid off) with the option to purchase health insurance through the employer's group plan for up to 18 months after employment ends. From the time *COBRA* was passed in 1985, the departing employee has been responsible for paying 102% of the cost of the premiums to keep *group health insurance* in place under the former employer's health plan (*Continuation of Health*, n.d.). In 2009, Congress passed new laws that can extend the time period for *group health insurance* coverage under *COBRA* beyond 18 months in certain circumstances and also require the former employer to continue paying a large portion of the insurance premiums.

If a person loses a job and does not have *group health insurance* through another employer, it usually makes sense to keep the former employer's health plan for as long as possible.   Under the new laws passed in 2009, the continuation of a previous employer's *group health insurance* under COBRA should be more affordable than in the past, and if anyone in the person's immediate family has a *pre-existing condition* that would limit coverage under *individual private health insurance*, it would usually make sense to maintain the more comprehensive coverage under the former employer's *group health insurance* plan (*COBRA Continuation Coverage*, n.d.).

Additional Considerations about Insurance

If you have health insurance, even very good *group health insurance*, that does not necessarily mean that your healthcare needs will be inexpensive or worry free.

When our *pediatrician* and *neurologist* suggested that we start physical therapy to help Lynn develop her walking skills, we did not think much about the cost. At the time, Lynn had *individual private health insurance* coverage which we purchased when Lynn was only a couple months old. The *pediatrician*'s subsequent diagnosis of Lynn's *hypotonia* between 6 and 12 months was not considered a *pre-existing condition* because the diagnosis came after we started Lynn's *individual private health insurance* coverage. We presumed that physical therapy was common enough that the *individual private health insurance* would cover all or most of the expense of Lynn's physical therapy. After all, that is why we pay all those expensive *premiums*!

Unfortunately, when we actually inquired about how much of the physical therapy costs would be covered by insurance, we learned that physical therapy would not be covered at all, and we would have to pay the full cost of each visit out-of-pocket. This was due to an exclusion in our *individual private health insurance* policy for Lynn.

Luckily, around the same time, we were able to enroll the whole family on the *group health insurance* through Patrick's employer. Although Patrick's employer did not cover much of the monthly *premium* costs, the *premium* for the family's *group health insurance* still cost about the same as we were paying for *individual private health insurance*. We enrolled in the *group health insurance* because we were confident the coverage and benefits would be considerably better with the *group health insurance* than with the *individual private health insurance*. Were we correct? Yes and no.

Unlike with our *individual private health insurance*, physical therapy was "covered" under our new *group health insurance*, but before the insurance company would pay any portion of the physical therapy expenses, we had to meet a $3,000 "*deductible*" (this is the amount of money that an insured individual or family must pay out-of-pocket before the insurance company will begin paying an agreed portion of certain medical expenses). After we satisfied the $3,000 *deductible*, then the insurance company was supposed to pay 70% of the cost of each physical therapy visit. However, with our particular *group health insurance*, the insurance company also had a limit of 30 total therapy visits a year for an insured family member. After 30 visits in a given year, insurance would not cover any portion of the cost. Ironically, with weekly physical therapy visits costing about $100 per session, we realized that just over half-way through the year we would simultaneously meet our $3,000 out-of-pocket deductible (thereby allowing insurance benefits to begin) and meet the 30 visit limit for therapy sessions in a given year (thereby preventing any insurance benefits to be paid). Essentially, this meant that although physical therapy is covered by the *group health insurance*, we would receive no benefits.

Then, we learned that insurance did not distinguish between physical therapy, *occupational therapy*, speech therapy, or any additional therapy services Lynn may need. After Lynn had a total of 30 "therapy" visits in a year, then our *group health insurance* would not provide any benefits. When our *pediatrician* suggested that we start Lynn on occupational and speech therapy, this meant that we would reach our 30 total visits even sooner each year. This is just a single example of how insurance coverage limitations, even under *group health insurance* plans, can prevent coverage for certain necessary and even common medical expenses.

Another detail we failed to consider when we changed from *individual private health insurance* to *group health insurance* is what would happen if Patrick lost his job and his *group health insurance* and we were forced to go back to *individual private health insurance*. We had presumed that our switch from *individual private health insurance* to *group health insurance* through Patrick's job would provide better coverage and benefits, but as noted above, we quickly learned this was not true. From the standpoint of insurance costs and benefits, there was really little difference between Lynn's benefits under the initial *individual private health insurance* and benefits under our particular *group health insurance*. Then we realized that we had cancelled a decent *individual private health insurance* policy for Lynn that had no *pre-existing condition* limitations related to Lynn's *hypotonia* so that we could get *group health insurance* that turned out to provide no better benefits!

What would happen if Patrick lost his job and *group health insurance*? Unfortunately, since Patrick worked for a small firm with less than 20 employees, the *COBRA* rules would not apply, and the company would not be required to offer Patrick *group health insurance* coverage under *COBRA* as discussed above. At best, Patrick would have only a few months of continued *group health insurance*. This means if Patrick lost his job and we needed health insurance for Lynn, we would need to get *individual private health insurance* again. However, any new *individual private health insurance* for Lynn would consider her *hypotonia* a *pre-existing condition*, and most of the doctor visits that Lynn actually needed would no longer be covered!! If this job loss situation had actually happened, then the move to *group health insurance* (which yielded no real advantage) would have left us much worse off in the long run than simply continuing with the original *individual private health insurance*.

This example is not intended as a simple criticism of *individual private health insurance* or *group health insurance*. It is meant to highlight the importance of doing your homework and paying attention to the coverage details and costs of your current and prospective health insurance plan. Before you make any change to your insurance coverage, make sure that there will either be a meaningful drop in costs (i.e. lower *premiums*, lower *deductibles*, lower co-insurance payments after *deductibles* are met, etc.) and/or a considerable improvement to the benefits (i.e. fewer restrictions, no *pre-existing condition* limitations, etc.). Hopefully, you have comprehensive health insurance and have none of the same issues and concerns we have faced with insurance coverage. If you are facing similar issues, however, we hope you can learn something from some of our experiences.

Becoming Familiar with Health Insurance Coverage and Advocating for your Baby

Navigating healthcare is often difficult and confusing. It is extremely important to become familiar with your current health insurance coverage and with any coverage you may get in the future, so you can make informed decisions about your family's healthcare needs. You must read your insurance policy, learn the terminology used by the insurance company and learn how to read an *explanation of benefits*. You must read everything your insurance company sends you about benefits it has provided or claims it has rejected. If you receive a letter from your insurance company stating that a claim is "denied" or "not covered", you should always follow up with the insurance company and verify this is correct based on your policy. Always call the insurance company if you have any questions or believe there has been a mistake, and involve your employer or its human resources department if you believe the insurance company has made a mistake and is not cooperating with you to fix it (*You Are an Advocate*, n.d.).

As parents we are the best, and unfortunately sometimes the only, advocates for our children. For this reason you should learn as much as you can about your baby's diagnosis and keep complete and organized records of your doctor visits, related expenses and insurance benefits received. You may constantly be on the phone with your doctors and insurance companies trying to figure out why certain expenses are not being covered when you believe they should be. Make sure you write down the names of everyone you talk with and the dates of your conversations and keep that information with your other medical records (*You Are an Advocate*, n.d.). Make sure to get both sides of the story; one story from the doctor's office regarding what service was performed and what paperwork was filed with the insurance company, and one story from the insurance company about what paperwork was received and why it was not covered as filed.

In our experience, processing errors by someone at the doctor's office or someone at the insurance company was very often the reason for an insurance claim denial. If you simply accept these claim denials without following up to verify the denials are correct, you may be paying for medical expenses that should rightly be paid by the insurance company under your particular insurance plan. For example, we received a claim denial for a physical therapy visit stating that we had exceeded our 30 visits per calendar year. We were certain this was incorrect because it was only January, and we had only seen the *physical therapist* **two times**. However, it required a 30-minute call from Elisabeth to the insurance company to address the problem, and the problem still continued for several weeks until a computer glitch could be corrected. You should learn about the claims appeal process and what steps you can take to try to get rejected claims covered. Your doctor's office staff can be a very helpful resource when dealing with this process.

When dealing with insurance companies and planning for your medical expenses, you might as well get the most "bang for your buck". Many people must satisfy a *deductible* before insurance benefits will cover all or a portion of certain medical expenses. In Lynn's case, medical expenses such as physical therapy, an *MRI* and related hospitalization, blood work, her *DAFOs* and certain other expenses would not be covered until we satisfied an annual *deductible*. If you have any control over the timing of medical procedures and expenses, you might consider scheduling these procedures in the current calendar year so that if you have already paid your full *deductible*, you will maximize the insurance benefits received in connection with your out-of-pocket *deductible* payment. This suggestion also highlights the importance of being proactive and getting involved in your baby's development as soon as you identify a potential delay.

In our case, we paid our annual *deductible* in connection with certain medical expenses in November and December 2008, and then we had to pay our 2009 deductible in January 2009 to cover certain other large expenses for Lynn. With slightly better planning and coordination, we could have scheduled the January appointments and expenses in December to avoid having to pay another out-of-pocket *deductible* for those services we knew we would need anyway.

Please note this suggestion applies to accelerating the scheduling of later medical expenses into the current year to maximize the insurance benefits for your current *deductible*. We do not recommend the inverse in which you delay necessary medical treatment or expenses for several months or more to maximize the insurance benefits in connection with the next year's *deductible* payment.

Early Intervention Programs

When we told our *neurologist* about the gap in our insurance coverage for physical therapy, she suggested that we contact *Babies Can't Wait* to see if the program could provide assistance. She told us *Babies Can't Wait* is a statewide program in Georgia that could be a potential resource to help defray some expenses not covered by insurance, so we decided to research the program. We wanted to get physical therapy started soon, but the potential expense of the therapy warranted at least a little research.

We learned that *Babies Can't Wait* is Georgia's *Early Intervention Program* for infants and toddlers with disabilities. Each state has a similar program, and all are funded by the federal government under Part C of the *Individuals with Disabilities Education Act of 2004 (IDEA)*. IDEA provides federal funding to each state's respective *Early Intervention Program* to assist children with disabilities, developmental delays or risks of developmental delay up to the age of two or three, depending on the state program

(*Early Intervention Program*, n.d.). For 2009, the federal government has appropriated $436 million to fund *Early Intervention Program*s across the country, and in 2008, state *Early Intervention Programs* collectively served 321,894 children nationwide (*Annual Appropriations and Number,* n.d.). Each state's program is a little bit different but they all fall under the same general rules of Part C of *IDEA*. Part C of *IDEA* is intended to provide funding for services to assist children with physical, social, cognitive, communication and feeding delays. Some common services provided under state *Early Intervention Programs* include, for example, physical therapy, *occupational therapy*, speech therapy, audiology services, nutrition services and social work services (National Dissemination Center for Children with Disabilities, n.d.)

If you suspect your infant or toddler has a developmental delay, you should contact your state's *Early Intervention Program*. To find direct contact information for your state's *Early Intervention Program*, please visit our web site's parent resources page and follow the appropriate links. You should confirm the actual procedures of your state's program, but based on our research of *IDEA* and our experiences with <u>*Babies Can't Wait*</u> the process should be generally as follows.

Although it is best to talk with your *pediatrician* about working with your state's *Early Intervention Program*, you should not need a referral from your *pediatrician* in order for your state's *Early Intervention Program* to provide an evaluation. If services are approved after an evaluation, the *Early Intervention Program* will require a doctor's order, so having a letter from a doctor may speed the process. When you contact your state's *Early Intervention Program*, they will assign a service coordinator to assist you. Your service coordinator will set up your child's evaluation, and this evaluation will look at all aspects of your child's development. This evaluation should be done at your home and should be free of charge. You can expect this qualification process to take at least a couple weeks. If your child qualifies for the program, then appropriate people from your state's program will create an Individualized Family Service Plan with your input which will outline the services your child will receive. *Early Intervention Programs* are intended to place a strong emphasis on treating each child in his or her "natural environment" which means any therapy coordinated through the program will likely take place in your own home (National Dissemination Center for Children with Disabilities, n.d.). After our experience with <u>*Babies Can't Wait*</u>, we cannot overstate the importance and convenience of this aspect of the program.

Your child's qualification for the program should be based solely on his physical assessment and not on your income. Depending upon the procedures of your state's *Early Intervention Program*, the program may consider your income and insurance coverage to determine whether your family is eligible for financial assistance through the program to cover all or a portion of the costs of the services required for your baby. The program may use a sliding income scale to pro-rate how much you pay and how much the program pays for services based on your household income. The *Early Intervention Program* may be able to work with your insurance company so that any financial assistance provided by the program for your baby's services will count toward your annual insurance *deductible*. Again, you should talk with your state's *Early*

Intervention Program to confirm these details apply in your state (National Dissemination Center for Children with Disabilities, n.d.).

After researching the program, we contacted *Babies Can't Wait* to see if Lynn's condition and our insurance and financial circumstances allowed us to qualify for assistance through the program. In a matter of a few weeks, the program completed Lynn's physical assessment, reviewed our insurance and income details, and completed the rest of the qualification process. In addition to setting us up with a great *physical therapist*, the program ended up covering most of the expense of physical therapy! We strongly encourage you to look into your state's *Early Intervention Program*.

Parent Support Groups

It can be very difficult to adjust to the reality of your baby's developmental delay or possible permanent disability, and it requires time and support from others. Unless you have experienced it yourself, it is hard to truly understand how difficult it is to watch other children walking, running and playing while your baby's participation is limited by a physical delay or disability. Although we have emphasized the importance of being patient and resisting the urge to compare your child with others, these lessons take time and practice to learn. Parents with a child that has a developmental delay may find that the people they turn to first, their family and friends, are not able to provide the support they need. Sometimes family and friends, in an attempt to show support or cheer you up, may suggest or even argue emphatically that your baby's delayed development is nothing to be concerned about and it is perfectly normal. While these people may have the best intentions, this feedback is not always helpful or constructive. It can be extremely beneficial to communicate with other parents who are in a similar situation or have been through a similar situation in the past.

Parent to Parent is a government program that provides social and emotional support and informational resources to parents of children with disabilities by matching parents who have experience raising a child with the same development delay or disability. Each state has its own *Parent to Parent* program, and the programs are typically volunteer-based. Parents interested in helping others can volunteer with the program and receive training to become a "support parent". Support is usually provided over the phone, although some parents may choose to meet face-to-face (*What Is Parent to Parent,* n.d.).

Family Voices is a non-government program that promotes family-centered care for all children with disabilities or special healthcare needs. The organization has a national network that coordinates with other government and private organizations to "provide families with tools to make informed decisions, advocate for improved public and private policies, build partnerships among professionals and families, and serve as a trusted resource on healthcare" (*About Family Voices*, n.d.). There are *Family Voices* representatives in each state – some volunteer and some paid employees of *Family Voices* or other organizations in the network.

Online message boards can be another great way to get support from other people who have been through similar situations. Message boards also provide the safety of anonymity, so you can speak openly and honestly about your baby's situation and how it makes you feel without revealing private details about who you are. You can ask for advice or ask questions you may otherwise not feel comfortable directly asking others. You can find a message board for just about every condition and diagnosis out there. If you sign up for a message board, we recommend observing for a while before actively participating to determine if the environment and dialogue is right for you. It is also important to remember that you should not consider it a substitute for proper medical advice and evaluation. The information is not verified as accurate and should be reviewed with a medical professional. You should make sure the message board has a moderator who can filter out any inappropriate comments or participants. For Lynn's condition, Elisabeth found **Hypotonia Hope** in *Yahoo Groups* and **Hypotonia** on *iVillage*. Both of these groups have very active members. Even if you do not post any comments, you can still read through the messages to get some great ideas. If you do pose a question, you may get a response with some answers in as quick as a day.

We strongly encourage you to find a support group or person that you can talk to openly. Please visit our website's parent resources page for links to each of the programs mentioned above. Even if you have supportive family and friends, it can still be helpful to have someone else to turn to who can step back from the situation and give you an outside observer's attention and thought. Some of the best support is from a parent who has experienced a similar situation and can truly understand what you are feeling and going through. Good luck and please know that you are never alone.

Activities to Help Your Baby Walk

The remainder of this book offers a wide range of games and activities intended to help your baby learn to walk. These suggestions are based upon our experiences with Lynn throughout various stages in her walking development and our observations of what worked best for her and what she enjoyed the most. These games and activities are not intended as medical advice or as a substitute for seeing your *pediatrician* or *physical therapist*. Always check with your pediatrician prior to implementing any of these activities to make sure they are appropriate for your child. Ask your pediatrician whether your child should be evaluated by a pediatric *physical therapist*. It is important to note that these activities are not intended for children with severe developmental disabilities.

Whether your child is just a little behind or has been diagnosed with a condition that requires special attention, these activities offer fun ways to play and interact with your baby while working to improve strength, coordination, muscle control and balance. Of course, we cannot guarantee these activities will have your baby walking in no time, but these activities have worked for Lynn, and we sincerely hope they will work for your baby too.

Just to set expectations properly in advance, these activities may not amaze you from the standpoint of complexity or ingenuity. The activities are limited in complexity due to the limited nature of your baby's physical abilities and *gross motor skills*. In fact, you may see some games or activities that you already do with your baby. For each of these activities, we have tried to identify the aspects of the movements that are most helpful for improving your baby's development of walking skills and related muscles. It does not require intense or acrobatic activities to make progress, and even these small or simple activities can still be challenging and beneficial for your baby. To maximize the benefits of these activities, you should 1) emphasize proper form in each motion, and 2) work the activities into a consistent daily routine and practice, practice, practice.

When working these activities into your daily routine, it is vitally important to make these activities fun and exciting for your baby by incorporating toys, games, songs and other creative devices. If your baby views these activities as "work" instead of "play", then your baby may not want to cooperate. If your baby cries or protests during a particular activity, then move on and try something else. Attention spans can be very short, so have multiple activities in mind and be flexible in moving from one to the other. Do not plan marathon training sessions. The hardest part is keeping their attention and enthusiasm, so be sure to provide lots of positive feedback and congratulations for making efforts and for successful completions.

For most activities, we have suggested one or more products or toys that may make the activity more fun or effective for your baby. Please visit our web site's toys and products page for a full list of products we have found helpful in these activities. We have made these products available for purchase on our web site (in association with Amazon.com) and we have indicated on the web site the activity number(s) for which each product or toy is helpful. In recommending toys we have been conscious of varying budgets and have included toys in different price ranges. You may also consider shopping at discount stores to find inexpensive toys and products that can add novelty to activities without breaking your budget. Even products as simple and inexpensive as stickers and coloring books can be very helpful for keeping your baby's attention. Since babies reach milestones at different ages, some of the toys we have suggested in the activities may not be age appropriate for your baby. Please take your baby's age and development into consideration when making toy selections.

As you work with your baby throughout the day, ask yourself "How can I make this game or activity more beneficial for my baby?" Pay attention to how your baby moves, and make sure your baby maintains good posture and joint alignment during the activities. For example, make sure your baby is not pointing his feet inward or outward or rolling his ankles in or out. We constantly corrected Lynn's feet while she was playing to keep her right foot from pointing out to her right side. Remember to stay within reach of your baby at all times during these activities to help with these posture and alignment corrections and also to minimize the risk of falling or injury.

Remember to be persistent as you introduce new games and activities to your baby. Do not just try an activity once and then abandon your efforts if your baby protests or is not excited about the activity. You may have to repeat the activities several times over a series of days or weeks before your baby catches on. Once your baby does catch on, you may be surprised by how quickly certain ideas fall into place. For example, we started introducing Lynn to baby sign language when she was about 8 months, and it took about 3 months before Lynn really started understanding the connection between the words, ideas and signs we were teaching her. Once she started making the connection, she was so excited, and it was easier to teach her other signs. Some neighborhood friends mentioned that they had tried to teach their baby to sign, but it was hopeless. They said they tried for 2 weeks, but it was clear it would never work. You have to be realistic about your baby's abilities, persistent in your efforts, and patient with the gradual progress.

We understand that helping your baby to walk is a gradual process, so we have grouped these activities into five levels of generally ascending difficulty. We defined each level according to what your baby can do independently based on his own gross motor skills, fine motor skills and cognitive abilities. Always check with your *pediatrician* prior to implementing any of these activities to make sure they are appropriate for your child.

Level 1 – Sits independently and starting to pull to standing.
Level 2 – Pulls to standing, stands with support and crawls.
Level 3 – Cruises holding on to furniture.
Level 4 – Walks with support.
Level 5 – Attempts to stand alone and attempts a few steps alone.

These level descriptions do not necessarily mean you must introduce these activities in the order we have presented. Each baby will have different strengths and weaknesses, and your baby may find some activities easier or more enjoyable than others. However, it is important to work with your baby on a good mix of activities. This type of "cross-training" should help your baby develop and strengthen all the different muscle groups that must successfully work together for your baby to learn to walk. Also, your child must be developmentally ready to do these activities. The activities generally assume that your baby is not delayed in fine motor skills or cognitive development as this would affect your baby's ability to perform these activities. As a point of reference, Lynn was 15 months old when she began these activities with her physical therapist.

We have also included safety tips in many of the activities to alert you when you should use some general or specific precautions to prevent basic issues like your baby losing balance or falling.

As a final note, for simplicity and consistency we have used masculine terms (e.g. he, him, his, etc.) throughout our descriptions of these activities. However, none of these activities are intended to be more beneficial for a boy or a girl.

Level 1 – Sits Independently

The following activities are best suited for a baby who is able to sit independently and is beginning to pull himself up to standing.

Remember to take your baby's age and his physical and cognitive development into consideration when selecting toys to use during these activities. To be sure these activities are appropriate for your baby at this stage in his development, check with your *pediatrician* or *physical therapist* first.

1. Kick It

Starting Position: Have your baby lay down flat on his back with his legs stretched straight out on the floor or changing table. This activity also works well after a diaper change but can be done anywhere your baby can lay on his back.

Motion: Help him lift his knee up so his upper leg is pointing up to the ceiling and his lower leg is parallel with the floor or changing table. You may need to hold his upper leg in the upright position. Encourage him to kick his leg up in the air toward the ceiling. You can provide some resistance to his kick by placing your hand on top of his lower leg as he tries to kick up.

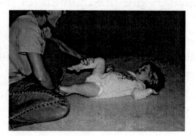

Muscles: This movement helps strengthen the leg muscles.

You can make this activity more fun by placing your baby on his back on a play mat or activity gym with hanging toys that he can kick.

2. Massage, Ankle Rolls and Foot Stimulation

Starting Position: There is technically no starting position for this activity, but it is so much fun that we could not help but include it. Your baby can begin by sitting or lying on the floor. You can use a small vibrating massager which you can purchase from most retail stores. If you need some ideas, check out our web site's product page for the one we used.

Motion: Turn on the massager and apply it to his arms, legs, feet, and back. This should just be a light gentle vibrating massage. This will help stimulate his muscles and increase blood flow to the area. If you are lucky maybe he will massage you back!

You can also do gentle ankle rolls with your baby and rub or tickle his feet. If your baby is anything like Lynn, his range of motion and flexibility is already there. The stimulation to the feet and ankles can help increase your baby's awareness and control of his ankles, feet and toes.

Safety Tip: Make sure you do not force his feet or ankles too far when doing rolls. You are not really stretching but trying to make your baby aware of what his feet can do and how to move his toes, feet and ankles for improved control.

Muscles: Massage and other types of stimulation increase blood flow to the areas being massaged or stimulated. This can be useful for a good warm-up or cool-down before or after other activities. This should also make your baby less sensitive to your touch as you work with him during activities.

You can make this activity more fun by:

    A. Giggling as you apply the massager and pretend you are tickling him.
    B. Letting him hold the massager and apply it to himself (with your supervision) or apply it to you.
    C. Singing the Hokey Pokey in connection with manipulating his feet and ankles.
    D. Playing "this little piggy" when you manipulate his feet and toes.

3. Dance, Baby, Dance

<u>Starting Position</u>: Turn on some fun music and hold your baby firmly in your arms while you stand.

<u>Motion</u>: Start dancing! Most babies seem to love music and dancing. We like swing dancing in our house. As you dance, your baby will have to use his muscles to stabilize his body. Change directions and start and stop as you go. You may not want to do this right after he eats! This is a good way to expose your baby to different types of music and help him develop a sense of rhythm and appreciation for music. You don't have to play "baby" music, so listen to something you like.

If your baby does not seem excited or seems a bit confused by the activity, dance with your spouse or a friend to demonstrate for your baby how much fun dancing can be.

<u>Safety Tip</u>: Be very careful of your surroundings and watch out for other people, furniture, walls, etc. Use your judgment to decide how much enthusiasm and vigor you should use while dancing based on your baby's development and age. Make sure you do not shake or jostle your baby. Your baby should be able to maintain good head control at all times.

<u>Muscles</u>: Dancing with your baby makes him use his *core* muscles which helps improve his balance and stability.

You can make this activity more fun by:

    A. Playing different types of music to see which type your baby likes best.
    B. Having other people join you to dance.

4. Joy Ride

Starting Position: Place your baby sitting upright in a wagon, and make sure your baby holds onto the sides of the wagon for stability and safety.   If you are doing this activity inside the house, you can also use a sturdy laundry basket with high sides.

Motion: Push or pull the wagon for a fun ride around your house, the driveway, the yard or a park. Go slowly at first and keep a close eye on your baby's ability to maintain his stable seated position. He will have to hold on to the sides and also use his *core* muscles to maintain his balance as you move him around. With any luck, he will be giggling and enjoying this activity in no time. As he becomes more familiar with this activity, you can include turns and figure eights, weave in and out of furniture if you are inside, and start and stop the ride (just not too abruptly).

We found that Lynn enjoyed the indoor rides in the laundry basket. She would even "help" us with our laundry so that she could get into the basket when it was empty and go for a ride. Encourage and assist your baby to use the sides of the basket to pull himself up to a standing position. Then help him as he lifts each leg up and over the side to climb in or out of the basket. Make sure you hold on to the basket while he pulls up and climbs in and out of the basket to be sure the basket does not tip.

Safety Tip: Your baby should be able to sit independently without assistance or difficulty before attempting this activity. Use your judgment as to the speed that is right. Do not go so fast that your baby is bumping against the sides of the wagon or basket as you turn, and obviously make certain he never falls out. While you should keep an eye on your baby to make sure he remains stable in the wagon or basket, you should also watch where you are going and be careful not to run into anything yourself. Use a wagon or basket that is not so large that your baby will slide around in it. Your baby should maintain his seated position and control of his head at all times.

Muscles: The sitting and riding aspect of this activity helps strengthen the *core* and improves balance. Climbing in and out of the wagon or basket should work the whole body.

You can make this activity more fun by:

   A. Playing red light, green light. Say out loud, "Green light" and begin the ride. Shout "red light!" and bring the ride to a stop (again, not too abruptly).
   B. Making car sounds. Beep at furniture in your way. Put your pretend turn signal on and beep as you reverse. "Rev" the pretend engine in the basket or wagon.
   C. Pick up stuffed animals for "carpool". Your baby can reach over the sides of the wagon or basket to pick up animals to strengthen his back and improve balance.

5. Diaper Change Sit Up

<u>Starting Position</u>: Have your baby lay down flat on his back with his legs stretched straight out on the floor or changing table. This motion will work fine anywhere your baby can lay flat, but as the name implies, we found this was a good habit to get into after a diaper change. Once your baby gets the hang of it, it is not a bad idea to use this motion as often as possible when you help him up from a laying position.

<u>Motion</u>: After changing your baby's diaper, use one hand to hold down his upper legs on the changing table just above his knees. Do not apply too much pressure to the legs; just enough so he does not lift off the table or floor. Make sure he does not arch his back. You may want to have him bend his knees to help keep his back on the floor. Encourage him to use his abdominal muscles to sit up. You may have to offer him your other hand so he can pull himself up. As his strength improves, he will not need as much assistance from you. Try to get him to repeat this a few times.

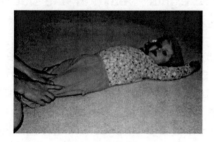 

If your baby cannot sit straight up, he may twist his upper body to one side and push himself up with a hand or arm. This is OK.   With practice, hopefully he will be able to sit straight up.

<u>Safety Tip</u>: As you repeat sit ups, make sure you help your baby lay back to a flat position. Whether on the changing table or the floor, do not let your baby simply fall back and hit his head. If your baby is on an elevated surface such as the changing table make sure you keep a firm grip on him.

<u>Muscles</u>: This is a great motion to strengthen the *abdominal muscles*. This also helps improve head and neck control especially for babies whose head drags behind when pulling up to a seated position.

You can make this activity more fun by:

    A. Holding a small toy just out of his reach and encouraging him to sit up for it.
    B. Trying the sit ups before putting his clothes back on while his stomach is exposed. Kiss or blow on his stomach to make him laugh and then work with him to sit up. Then help him lower back down to lying flat and repeat.
    C. Tickling your baby's feet or toes while holding his upper legs. He will probably want to sit up and see what is making his feet tickle.
    D. Having your baby sit up to give you a high five.

6. Row the Boat

Starting Position: Sit on the floor facing your baby with your legs out in front of you. Have your baby sit facing you in between your legs with his legs out in front of him. Extend your arms out in front of you and hold your baby's hands.

Motion: Lean back as you pull his arms towards you so that he is leaning forward and bent at the waist. Then push his arms back towards him as he leans his upper body backwards. Go back and forth in a rowing motion. As you lean back encourage him to try and "pull" you back up. When he leans back encourage him to pull himself back up with his arms.

As he gets stronger encourage him to lean back further to strengthen his abdominal muscles. He will have to use his abdominal and back muscles to sit up and control his body as he leans back. You can do a variation of this activity by having your baby hold on to one end of a towel and try to pull it away from you in a game of tug of war.

Safety tip: Do not push and pull your baby too hard. You do not want to make jerky movements and have your baby be unable to stabilize his body. Be careful not to extend his arms out too far.

Muscles: This activity strengthens the arms, shoulders, neck, and *abdominal* muscles.

You can make this activity more fun by:

A. Singing "Row your boat" as you do this. Lynn still sings this song all the time, even when we are not playing the game.
B. Singing the ABC's as you go back and forth.
C. Pretending you are stuck lying back and you need your baby to pull you back up.

7. Airplane / Superman

<u>Starting Position</u>: Lay on your back with your knees pointed toward the ceiling, bent at a 90 degree angle and your lower legs parallel with the floor. Hold your lower legs close together and place your baby face down on your lower legs with his tummy on your shins, his feet around your feet, and his head extended just beyond your knees. Hold both your baby's hands for stability.

<u>Motion</u>: Gently move your knees forward, backward and slightly to each side to give your baby the sensation of flying. Go slowly if your baby has not done this before. Help your baby learn to maintain balance by shifting his weight as you move your legs in different directions. Obviously, be very careful that your baby does not roll off your legs.

<u>Safety Tip</u>: In addition to those safety recommendations mentioned above, you should also remember that this activity places extra pressure on your baby's *abdomen*, back and chest. Your baby's breathing may be slightly more difficult from this position. Even if he still seems to be having fun, do not do this activity for more than a minute or so at a time. And if your baby has any other issues breathing (e.g. a cold, congestion, asthma, etc.), you may consider not doing this activity until the breathing issues resolve.

<u>Muscles</u>: This activity particularly strengthens your baby's back and abdominal muscles as he lift his head up and balances his body to look at you.

You can make this activity more fun by:

A. Singing him a song or making airplane sounds as you move.
B. Bending your knees and dropping your feet to the floor to lower your baby so his feet touch the floor, and then counting down to "blast off" to take him for another ride on the airplane.

8. Ride a Little Horsey

<u>Starting Position</u>: Sit on a chair or sofa with your knees bent, your legs together and your feet on the floor. Have your baby sit on your upper legs just above your knees facing towards you with his legs straddling your knees. Depending on the amount of support your baby needs, hold him securely on the waist or chest or by his arms with both of your hands.

<u>Motion</u>: Raise and lower your legs in a quick rhythmic motion by lifting and lowering your heels, and gently bounce your baby on your knees. As the tradition goes, sing "Ride a little horsey, up to town. Ride a little horsey, don't fall down." As you sing "don't fall down" lean him slightly to one side while still holding him securely, and then return him to an upright sitting position. Depending on your baby's *core* strength, you may need to assist him to return to an upright position. After he gets familiar with the game and the motion of returning to his seated position for another ride, he should do most of the work to return to his seat. Keep singing and alternating the sides you lean your baby to.

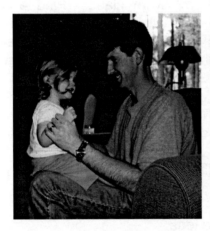

<u>Safety Tip</u>: Do not bounce your baby too hard while in the seated position. The bouncing motion will expand and compress his spine in the seated position, so you do not want to place too much pressure on the spine when bouncing. When you lean your baby to the sides, make sure you bring him to a gradual halt before returning him to an upright seated position. If you lean him to the side and stop suddenly, this could hurt his neck or back. You should consider your baby's development and ability to independently stabilize himself.

<u>Muscles</u>: This is a great activity to strengthen the *core* muscles. It helps to improve balance and stability.

9. Swim Lessons

<u>Starting Position</u>: Bring your baby into the pool with you for a swim. Hold him in your arms or place him in an inflatable baby float. See our web site's product page for suggestions of pool floats that are durable, fun and functional.

<u>Motion</u>: If you are holding your baby, sit him in your arms with his back up against your chest. If your baby is in a float, always keep a hand on him. Encourage him to kick his legs under the water. The water will add resistance to his legs and help strengthen them as he kicks. If you hold your baby, try holding him so he is lying with his back in the water and his belly facing up (i.e. back float position with you holding him) and encourage him to kick his legs. You can also try to flip him over and hold him under his belly so that his belly is in the water and his back is facing up. Of course, make sure his head remains up and above the water at all times.

<u>Safety Tip</u>: If you do not feel confident in the water with your baby, consider signing up for a parent-assisted baby swim class. Find a certified swim instructor who will help make you and your baby more comfortable in the water. Whenever you are in the pool, there should always be a lifeguard on duty.

You should always have a secure grip on your baby while in the pool. An inflatable baby float is not a lifesaving device and is not a substitute for a parent.

You can also put a Coast Guard approved life vest on your baby while you are in the water for added safety.

<u>Muscles</u>: Kicking in the water strengthens the legs.

You can make this activity more fun by:

A. Pretending you are a motor boat and having your baby help motor you around.
B. Having your baby kick floating pool toys.
C. Having your baby try to "race" another person playing with you in the pool.

10. Bend and Pick Up

<u>Starting Position</u>: Have your baby sit on a low stool or aerobic step with his feet flat on the floor and a little more than shoulder width apart with knees bent at a 90 degree angle. Encourage good posture in this seated position.

<u>Motion</u>: Place a toy or other object on the floor between his feet. Encourage him to bend at the waist and pick up the toy or object. Then, have him return to an upright seated position. During this motion, he should remain seated and keep his feet on the floor for balance and to help himself push back to an upright seated position. You should begin with a small toy or object, perhaps that he can grab with one hand while using the other hand for balance and stability as he returns to an upright position. As his strength increases, you can try larger objects (not necessarily heavy objects!!) that may require both hands to hold so it focuses more on the targeted muscle groups.

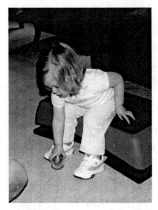

After your baby is able to stand from a seated position, you can modify this activity to have him pick up the toy from the floor and then stand up to place the toy in a bag that you hold in front of him just out of his reach. As he stands, remember to help him keep his feet and knees pointed forward and have him push through his legs to a standing position.

<u>Muscles</u>: This motion strengthens the back muscles. A strong back will help promote good posture and balance.

You can make this activity more fun by:

A. Placing a piece of food (e.g. a cracker or piece of cereal) on the floor so he can pick it up and eat it. Note: Obviously make sure the floor is clean and be sure he chews and swallows the food before repeating the motion to avoid any choking risk.
B. Putting a sticker on top of your baby's foot and asking him to take it off his foot and stick it on your shirt.
C. Placing a small stuffed animal on the floor and have him pick it up and hug it.

11. Do the Twist

Starting Position: Have your baby sit on a low stool or aerobic step with his feet flat on the floor and a little more than shoulder width apart with knees bent at a 90 degree angle. Encourage good posture in this seated position.

Motion: Sit in front of your baby and place objects on the stool or step on his right side. Encourage him to stay seated with his feet on the floor and twist to the right to reach the object and pick it up. Have him give the toy back to you, and then place the object on the stool or step to his left side. Repeat the motion on the left.

You should begin with a small object and place it very close to his sides. As his strength, balance and range of motion improves, you can try slightly bigger objects and place them farther away to his sides and toward the back corner of the stool or step. This requires your baby to make a larger trunk rotation and demands better balance to maintain the seated position through the movement. Remember to help your baby keep his feet on the floor and rear end on the step.

Muscles: This motion strengthens the *oblique abdominal muscles*. A strong abdomen helps him to maintain good posture and the balance needed to walk. This motion should also strengthen the muscles through the hips and buttocks.

You can make this activity more fun by:

    A. Picking up shapes to his side and placing them in a shape sorter in front of him or to his opposite side.
    B. Picking up jumbo puzzle pieces and placing them back in the jumbo peg puzzle in front of him or to his opposite side.
    C. Passing a ball back and forth to a person sitting on either side of him.

12. Squish It

<u>Starting Position</u>: Have your baby sit on a low stool or aerobic step with his feet flat on the floor and a little more than shoulder width apart with knees bent at a 90 degree angle. Encourage good posture in this seated position.

<u>Motion</u>: Place an object between his feet such as a small plush animal, a squeaky toy, or a pillow. The object should be something that is durable and will give way somewhat under pressure. Have him place one of his feet on the object and encourage him to push down to squish the object with his foot. This may be a strange movement, so you will probably have to guide him through this motion until he gets the hang of it. It is okay for him to lean forward to put more force into his legs but be sure he does not lift himself from the seated position. Then have him repeat with the other foot.

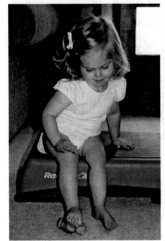

<u>Safety Tips</u>: Be careful about the objects you place under his feet. Obviously do not use anything you think may break under the pressure of his foot, and do not use anything with sharp edges that may poke your baby's foot when he applies pressure. You also do not want him twisting an ankle or knee by trying to push down or attempt to stand on an unstable object that may shift suddenly under his feet.

Hold on to the objects as he pushes down with his feet to prevent sudden shifting. Even after he gets the hang of this motion and eventually learns to stand, you should not try to have him stand up on an unstable or odd shaped object.

<u>Muscles</u>: This motion strengthens the legs and will help your baby with the muscles needed to stand from a seated position.

You can make this activity more fun by:

A. Using small toys that squeak or make sounds when squeezed.
B. Having him push his foot into a block of play dough (potentially messy), Silly Putty (less messy), or a block of memory foam (no mess) so that he can see his footprint. Supervise your baby closely and do not allow him to play with these items unsupervised. Make sure that your baby does not put any of these things in his mouth.

13. Bouncing on the Ball

<u>Starting Position</u>: Sit your baby on top of a large inflatable exercise ball. Hold your baby securely in this seated position with both your hands on his upper legs or around his waist for the best stability. You can position yourself either in front of him or behind him. Please remember that your baby should be able to sit independently before you attempt this activity. We recommend that you have another person to help stabilize the ball.

If you do not already have an exercise ball, see our web site's product page for exercise balls of different sizes, shapes and colors.

<u>Motion</u>: Gently press down on your baby's lap and upper legs to bounce him up and down on the exercise ball in a seated position.   His rear end should not leave the exercise ball, but simply press him down into the ball and let the ball raise him back up. It may take a few tries before he is comfortable with this motion.   After your baby becomes accustomed to this activity, he should be able to help balance himself and use his own body weight to help the bouncing motion.

<u>Safety Tip</u>: Your baby's sitting position on this activity is naturally unstable. If you have any concerns about your baby's ability to do this activity or your ability to keep him stable on the exercise ball, then ask your spouse or a friend to help you keep your baby stable or try another activity. Always make sure you are in a good position to stabilize him if he should lose his balance and begin to fall off the ball. Make sure you are a safe distance from any furniture or objects that may hurt your baby if you bump into them.

<u>Muscles</u>: This motion will require your baby to use various muscles throughout his hips, *abdomen* and back to maintain balance and his seated position.

You can make this activity more fun by:

    A. Putting on some music or singing a song and bouncing to the music or song.
    B. Letting your baby hold a toy or stuffed animal so he can make the toy or animal bounce with him.

Level 2 – Pulls up to Standing

The following activities are best suited for a baby who is able to pull himself up to standing, stand with support, and crawl.

Remember to take your baby's age and his physical and cognitive development into consideration when selecting toys to use during these activities. To be sure these activities are appropriate for your baby at this stage in his development, check with your *pediatrician* or *physical therapist* first.

14. Throw a Ball

<u>Starting Position</u>: Sit on the floor facing your baby with several feet in between him and you. Have your baby sit with his back straight and his legs out in front of him with his legs slightly apart. Alternatively, you can have him sit on a low stool or aerobic step with his feet flat on the floor to encourage good posture.

<u>Motion</u>: Give your baby a ball and assist and encourage him to hold the ball with both hands, raise it over his head and throw it across the room. He will have to use his *abdominal* muscles to stabilize himself in an upright position as he throws the ball. At first, you should use a relatively small ball, but as he becomes stronger you can use a larger ball with a little more weight to it. Try finding a small rubber playground ball (i.e. not a heavy medicine ball). You can also have him stand leaning back against a wall for support. Throw the ball gently back to him. He may not be able to catch it, but it may roll into his arms.

<u>Safety Tip</u>: Make sure that there is nothing nearby that may be knocked down by a wild throw that could hurt someone.   Your baby may also lose his balance when doing this activity so keep him away from items that he could fall on.

<u>Muscles</u>: This activity strengthens the arms and abdominal muscles.   It also helps improve balance and coordination.

You can make this activity more fun by:

- A. Having him try to throw the ball in a basket.
- B. Having several balls in play, and as he throws a ball to you, you throw a ball back to him.
- C. Having more than one other person throwing the ball with him so that he must rotate to face in different directions to throw the ball to one person and then to another.

15. Stand up at the Table

<u>Starting Position:</u> Have your baby sit on a low stool or aerobic step in front of a coffee table or other sturdy piece of furniture about 18 to 24 inches high. He should be facing the table and the front edge of the step or stool should be about 12 inches away from the table. As with other starting positions, his feet should be flat on the floor a little more than shoulder width apart and knees bent at a 90 degree angle.

<u>Motion:</u> Place a toy on the coffee table just out of his reach. Assist him to use his arms to hold the table to steady him and to use his legs to push up to standing at the table to get the toy. Make sure he gets the toy as a reward for his effort. Then have him lower back down to the step or stool and repeat. Try to help him lower to the step in a slow controlled manner rather than just dropping down on his bottom. This controlled lowering motion may take some time to develop.

As he improves, have him try holding the table with only one hand. This reduces his ability to pull up with his arms and requires him to focus on pushing up with his legs. When first attempting this motion, consider raising the level of the stool or step (the adjustable step comes in handy for this), so the standing motion is less difficult, but it must be low enough for him to start with his feet on the floor. As he improves with this motion, lower the step to increase the difficulty.

As with the other activities, pay attention to his legs and feet during the standing motion and while he is standing. Make sure his feet and knees are aligned and pointed straight in front of him. If they are not, correct the direction of his feet and make sure his hips are square to the table. Using correct form in this motion and all other activities should help reduce unnecessary stress on the joints.

<u>Safety Tip:</u> Make sure the table is sturdy enough not to tip when your baby pulls up on it, and do not use a table with a glass or detachable top. Keep your hands on your baby at all times until he is very comfortable with this activity to prevent falling and possible injury on the edge of the table. Place edge guards on the table for added safety.

<u>Muscles:</u> This motion is a full body strengthening move. It helps improve coordination between the arms and legs which will be helpful later when coordinating all the body movements needed to walk.

You can make this activity more fun by:

A. Placing a small toy piano keyboard on the table for him to play.
B. Placing small blocks on the table for him to stack.
C. Having him stand to turn pages in a book.

16. Stand Up!

<u>Starting Position</u>: Once your baby is confident using the table to pull himself to standing you can try this activity. Have your baby sit on a low stool or aerobic step in the middle of a room. Your baby should be able to rest his feet flat on the floor with his knees bent at a 90 degree angle and feet a little more than shoulder width apart. This will help promote proper body alignment. Try to keep his feet pointed straight in front of him to work the intended muscles. Encourage your baby, and assist him if necessary, to keep his back straight as he sits. Help him keep that straight posture throughout the motion.

<u>Motion</u>: From this seated position, encourage and assist your baby to stand up. Sit in front of him on the floor, and let him pull up on your shoulders or hand. Help him to sit down on the step making sure he lowers slowly rather than dropping to sit. As your baby progresses he will need less assistance from you. You can offer less assistance by keeping your hands lower, so instead of pulling himself up to your hands, he is steadying himself on your hands but pushing himself up with his legs. Eventually he should be able to stand up on his own and grab on to you for balance once he is standing.

<u>Muscles</u>: This motion strengthens the legs and helps to improve balance.

You can make this activity more fun by encouraging him to stand to:

    A. Place shapes in a shape sorter.
    B. Turn pages in an interactive lift the flap book.
    C. Take puzzle pieces in and out of a jumbo peg puzzle.
    D. Put a ball into a basket or bowl or throw bean bags into a box.
    E. Place stickers on a piece of paper or on your shirt. (Make sure your baby does not put the stickers in his mouth).
    F. Place a hat on your head or take it off.

The 5 position aerobic step shown in the pictures is a perfect tool for many of the activities we discuss. You can adjust it to different heights depending on the size of your child and the requirements of the particular activity.

As your baby gains strength and balance you can use a soft foam block instead of a hard step or stool. Since the foam is not as rigid as the step, your baby will have to rely more on his legs, balance and smaller stabilizer muscles to stand up. See the product page on our web site to look at the step and foam blocks we used.

17. Twist at the Table

<u>Starting Position</u>: Have your baby stand facing the coffee table or other sturdy piece of furniture holding on to it with both hands. Make sure his feet are flat on the floor and about shoulder width apart, and he is stable. His feet should be pointing forward toward the table with his hips square to the table.

<u>Motion</u>: Hold a small object out to his right side and slightly behind him. Encourage him to take the object from you by letting go of the table with his right hand and turning his upper body to reach and grab the object. Have him return to center facing the table and place the object on the table. Then hold the object out to his left side and slightly behind him and have him let go of the table with his left hand to turn his upper body to grab the object then return to center. Repeat several times. As  he becomes more comfortable letting go with one hand, hold the object further away and encourage him to turn his lower body and take a step toward you to reach the object. This is fine as long as he stays on his feet.

This activity is similar to its seated variation discussed earlier, but the objective here is slightly different. In addition to the strengthening benefits, the act of releasing the table helps to improve his balance and builds his confidence in his ability to stand with less assistance and outside support. The action of standing, stepping and grabbing an object also improves coordination between arms and legs.

<u>Safety Tip</u>: Make sure to watch him closely when he lets go of the table especially if he has not yet begun letting go with one hand while cruising. Make sure the object you give to your baby is small enough for him to grab with one hand and not heavy enough to throw off his balance and cause him to fall. Make sure the table or furniture he is holding is sturdy and will not tip under your baby's weight.

<u>Muscles</u>: This motion works the *core* muscles. This motion also improves torso flexibility, balance and confidence.

You can make this activity more fun by:

A. Having him take a ball from you and placing it in a busy ball train. (See our product page on the web site.)
B. Having him take a Mr. Potato Head part from you and put it in Mr. Potato Head on the table.
C. Having him take nesting toys from you and put them together. (See our product page.)

18. Twist and Stoop

<u>Starting Position</u>: Have your baby stand facing the coffee table holding on to it with both hands. Make sure his feet are flat on the floor and about shoulder width apart, and he is stable. His feet should be pointing forward toward the table with his hips square to the table.

<u>Motion</u>: Place a toy on a low stool or aerobic step to his right side. The height of the stool or step should place the toy at least several inches beyond his reach from his standing position. Encourage him to let go of the table with his right hand while slightly bending his knees to squat and grab the toy. He should not just bend at the waist to grab the toy without bending his knees. Have him return to a fully upright standing position. Alternate sides and repeat several times.

When you are first trying this activity, do not place the toy too low on a step or on the floor. If the toy is too low, he will just sit down to get it instead of bending at the knees and using his leg muscles to crouch and reach the toy. As he becomes more comfortable with the motion, place the toy lower and encourage deeper squats to reach the toy.

<u>Safety Tip</u>: Make sure as he leans forward to squat and reach the toy that he does not lose his balance and fall face forward onto the toy, step or floor. Encouraging him to bend at the knees instead of at the waist can help prevent the face forward fall. Make sure the table he is holding is sturdy and will not tip under your baby's weight.

<u>Muscles</u>: This activity strengthens the leg and *core* muscles. It also improves balance and coordination.

You can make this activity more fun by:

A. Placing some common items found in a diaper bag or purse on the step stool. Have him grab the items and return them to the purse or bag sitting on the table in front of him.

B. Having your baby stand at a play kitchen. Make sure the kitchen is sturdy and will not tip under his weight. Have him squat slightly to put food in the refrigerator or oven. See our web site for examples of play kitchens.

C. Having him pick up food items to place in a picnic basket on the table.

19. Might as Well Jump…

<u>Starting Position</u>: Sit your baby in a jumper. You can use one that hangs from a doorway or a free standing jumper. See our web site for suggestions. His feet should touch the floor completely with his legs slightly bent.

<u>Motion</u>: Play some music and encourage your baby to jump. Make sure that he is bending his knees to absorb the impact on the floor. If you do not have a jumper you can hold him under his arms and help him jump on the floor. This can also provide a good arm workout for you. Another option is going to an indoor play center that has giant inflatables for kids to play in. Remember the "moon bounce"? Find a place that divides the inflatables by age range so that your 18 month old is not getting jumped on by a 7 year old. Make sure that you are allowed to go into the inflatable to assist your baby. Also go when it is not crowded.

We took Lynn to one of these places and she absolutely loved it. We were not sure how much she would be able to do considering she could only crawl at the time. She was able to crawl up and down little hills and go through tunnels. She also enjoyed sitting there and bouncing up and down. Just sitting in the inflatable makes you tighten your muscles to keep your balance on the bouncy surface. Your baby will have to constantly use his muscles to stabilize himself. This is a great workout.

<u>Safety Tip</u>: If you use a jumper make sure that your baby does not exceed the weight or height limit. When using one that hangs from a doorway, hang it in an extra wide doorway so your baby does not run into the door frame or anything else in the room. He should be able to sit up independently for a while before you try this. Playing in an inflatable also requires that your baby is able to crawl and is able stabilize himself independently. You will need to supervise him closely. If he falls in the soft surface, he may have a difficult time getting back up and he may need your help.

<u>Muscles</u>: Jumping works most of the leg muscles.

You can make this activity more fun by:

  A. Holding your baby's favorite toys above him just out of his reach and having him jump up to get them.
  B. Playing music and encouraging your baby to jump to the music.

20. London Bridge is Falling Down

<u>Starting Position</u>: Have your baby lie flat on his back on the floor. Help him bend his knees and place his feet flat on the floor just next to his bottom. His feet should be about 6 inches apart for increased stability. Place his arms down by his sides with his palms down on the floor.

<u>Motion</u>: Encourage and assist your baby to lift his hips off the floor toward the ceiling. Have him push through his feet and legs and squeeze his bottom to raise his back off the floor. He can use his hands as well to help him push up and stabilize. It may take a while for him to understand what you want him to do and for him to build up the strength to lift himself. You can help him by placing your hand under his bottom or back and supporting his weight until he is able to support his weight independently. Help him to maintain this position in a controlled manner. You may also find it helpful to demonstrate this motion for him. Once our daughter got the hang of this motion, she loved doing it.

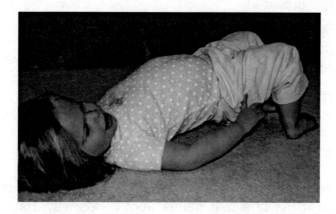

<u>Safety Tip</u>: Make sure your baby does not put too much pressure on his neck when he pushes his hips up. Do this activity on the floor and not on an elevated surface.

<u>Muscles</u>: This activity strengthens muscles in the lower back and *abdomen*. It also targets the muscles in the back of the legs. This activity also helps with balance.

You can make this activity more fun by:

   A. Doing this during a diaper change. Have him help you by lifting his bottom up so that you can slide the old diaper out and the new diaper under him and put it on. This creates a natural opportunity for multiple repetitions of the motion.

   B. Rolling a ball or car under his bottom when he lifts it off the floor. You can sing the popular nursery rhyme "London Bridge" while you are doing this. Be sure that you do not roll an object or toy underneath him that might be painful if he drops his hips too early and lands on it.

   C. Taking turns and letting him roll the ball or car under you also.

21. Fetch

<u>Starting Position</u>: Sit on the floor with your baby. Place toys around the room at varying distances.

<u>Motion</u>: Point to a toy and ask him to get it for you or roll a ball across the floor for him to get and throw back to you. Have your baby crawl, scoot, cruise, or walk depending on his development to get the toy and bring it back to you. Name the toy and use a lot of descriptive words when you ask him to get the toy. This will also help to build his vocabulary. When he brings it back to you make sure you praise him and play with the toy before you send him on his next mission.

We are not saying to treat your baby like a dog. Babies love to get things and proudly bring them back to show you. (Sometimes it's something you'd rather not have, like a dead bug!) The more your baby moves, the more he will get accustomed to getting where he wants to go by himself. It will build his endurance, strength, confidence and independence.

<u>Muscles</u>: This activity improves overall strength and endurance. It also helps improve balance and coordination.

You can make this activity more fun by:

    A. Having your baby go pick out a book to read from a shelf and bring it back to you.
    B. Having your baby go get his shoes and bring them to you to put them on him.
    C. Having your baby help clean up his toys and bring them back to a toy basket.

22. The Reach

<u>Starting Position</u>: Have your baby get in a four point crawl position on his hands and knees in front of a stool, aerobic step or a piece of furniture with a low shelf. Place a toy on the stool, step or shelf which should be about level with his shoulders (while in the crawling position) or slightly higher.

<u>Motion</u>: Encourage your baby to lift one arm and grab the toy off the stool with his hand while keeping his other hand and knees on the floor for balance. You want his arm to be fully extended and reaching upward so that he is engaging his arm, shoulder and back muscles when grabbing the toy. You can then have him return to the four point crawl position.

Then have your baby lift the toy off the floor and return it to the stool, step or shelf. Have him repeat this motion with each arm several times.

Your baby may try to find an easier way of getting the toys he wants rather than going through the motions suggested. Work with your baby to try to hold this position. If he puts up a fight, just move on to another activity.

<u>Safety Tips</u>: When he lifts one arm and reaches forward, he could lose his balance or his supporting arm might not be strong enough to hold all his weight. Make sure you keep a close eye on him and do not let him fall on his face or into the furniture. Make sure that if he leans on a piece of furniture to reach for a toy, the furniture will not tip.

<u>Muscles</u>: This motion targets the muscles in the arms, shoulders, neck and back.

You can make this activity more fun by:

    A. Placing a ring stacker on the stool or shelf in front of him and having him pick up rings from the floor next to him to stack on the ring. (See our product page on the web site.)
    B. Placing a shape sorter on the stool or shelf in front of him and having him pick up shapes from the floor to put into the shape sorter.
    C. Picking up a ball from the floor and placing it in a basket out in front of him.

23. Climb Every Mountain

<u>Starting Position</u>: Place a low stool or aerobic step in front of a chair or sofa. The step should be pushed flush against the front of the chair or sofa. Your baby should sit on the floor on the opposite side of the step from the chair.

<u>Motion</u>: Have your baby climb from the floor to the step and then from the step to the chair. Proper form in this motion is important to work his targeted muscle groups and prevent placing extra pressure on his knees.

Make sure that as he climbs onto the step (and chair), he first places his hands on the step above him and rises to his knees. Next, he should place one foot flat on the floor and push through his leg to get to his feet. His foot should be pointing forward toward the step, and his knee should be aligned and pointing in the same direction as his toes. Try not to let his foot point off to one side. Then he should place one of his knees on the step and use his arms to help pull himself onto the step and his other leg to push himself up. Repeat this motion to move from the step to the chair and try to alternate which leg goes up to the next level and which stays down for balance and pushing up.

What goes up must come down, so try to help your baby make a controlled descent from the chair to the step to the floor. As he comes down from the chair, make sure he comes down facing the chair on his belly. Help him reach his foot down to the step and then lower the other foot to stand on the step. Help him move slowly down into a seated position on the step, and then help him move in the same way to the floor. You will have to assist him to make a smooth descent.

<u>Safety Tip</u>: When you are done with this activity, remove the step from in front of the chair so that your baby cannot climb onto the step and the chair when your back may be turned. Be sure to assist your baby on the descent if he has not yet learned the concept

or fear of falling. Lynn used to love to slide backwards off a chair or bed and drop (luckily not too far) to the floor.

<u>Muscles</u>: This motion is a full body strengthening move. It emphasizes leg muscles as he pushes up and lowers back down and also works his arms as he pulls himself onto the chair.

You can make this activity more fun by:

A. Putting a toy farm animal up on the chair to encourage your baby to crawl up to get it and bring it back to the toy farm house on the floor. You can sing "Old MacDonald" and teach animal names as you do this.
B. Place pieces of a doll's clothing up on the chair and have your baby bring them down to dress the baby on the floor.
C. Place snacks on the chair so he gets a treat for reaching the top (make sure he has chewed and swallowed his food before coming down from the chair).

24. Stair Climber

<u>Starting Position</u>: Have your baby kneel on the floor in front of a set of stairs with his hands on the first step.

<u>Motion</u>: Assist your baby to crawl up a few stairs using the following form. Have him place his right foot flat on the floor next to his left knee with his toes pointing forward and his right knee pointing straight over his toes. Have him push up through his right foot and straighten his right leg so he comes to standing with his hands still on the first step.

Help him maintain proper alignment with his toes and knee pointing forward. After standing, help him move his hands up to the next step. Then have him lean forward and place his left knee on the first step and bring his right knee up to meet it so that he is now kneeling on the first step.

Now have him place his left foot flat on the step with toes pointed forward. Have him push through his left leg up to standing and move his hands to the next step up. Climb a few stairs and try to alternate the legs used to stand. When he comes back down the stairs, have him face the steps. Do not let him slide down on his bottom facing away from the steps towards the stairs below him. Have him move slowly down the stairs placing one foot, and then the other, on the step below. He should lower to his knees and then reach down for the step with the other foot.

<u>Safety Tip</u>: Remember to always supervise your baby on the stairs. Be sure you have a hand on his body at all times to catch him if he loses balance and to provide assistance as needed. You should always watch your baby from the steps below rather than from above. If you have stairs in your house, place safety gates at the top and bottom of your stairs to prevent your baby from sneaking on to the steps when your back may be turned.

<u>Muscles</u>: This activity works his whole body and targets the leg muscles. He also uses his arms to pull to the next step and maintain his balance. This is a great confidence builder.

You can make this activity more fun by:

A. Having one person above the baby on the steps cheering and encouraging the progress to the next step while another is spotting the baby from below and correcting his form.

B. Tossing a toy up a few steps so your baby can go get the toy. After allowing your baby to enjoy the toy for a moment once reaching it, let the toy fall down the steps to the floor below, so you have to go down and get it.

25. Obstacle Course

<u>Starting Position</u>: Create a baby obstacle course in a room in your home by placing pillows, couch cushions and a low stool or step on the floor for your baby to crawl and climb over. Space the obstacles 1 – 2 feet apart. Consider draping a blanket over two chairs or between the coffee table and sofa to create a tunnel. You can also make a large cardboard box into a tunnel by opening the top and bottom of the box.

<u>Motion</u>: Encourage your baby to move through the obstacle course you have laid out for him. Be creative and help your baby move in different ways through the obstacle course. Hold his hands and help him try to walk up and down over a stool or step. Allow him to crawl up and over large couch cushions or through tunnels you have set up. When he is through the course, make him come back through in reverse. You can modify the order or the number of the obstacles as he is moving through so it seems like one continuously changing obstacle course. As much as possible, you should encourage him to use his legs to push up and over obstacles.

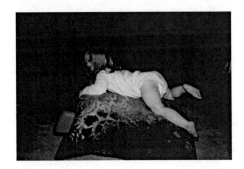
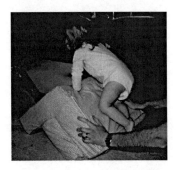

By spacing your obstacles 1 – 2 feet apart, you allow your baby to climb over one obstacle and get to the floor where he can be stable. Then he can tackle the next obstacle.

There are large soft activity blocks and tunnels that you can purchase to create a more colorful, exciting and challenging obstacle course. Check the toys and products page of our web site for examples and recommendations.

<u>Safety Tip</u>: Supervise your baby closely through the obstacle course. If you are using pillows or cushions, make sure he does not get stuck in any part of the course in a position where his face may be pointed down in a pillow or cushion for an extended period. Spacing obstacles a couple feet apart helps prevent getting stuck.

<u>Muscles</u>: This will depend upon the obstacles you set up, but it is generally a fun way to get your baby moving and strengthen him all over.

You can make this activity more fun by:

A. Getting down on the floor and going through the obstacle course with him.
B. Playing peek-a-boo as he comes around the corner of a piece of furniture.
C. Pulling a pull toy through the course for him to chase.
D. Placing a sturdy object under a large couch cushion or pillow. If the cushion is somewhat rigid, this will create a "seesaw" for your baby to climb over (be careful he does not fall when the seesaw tips down). If the cushion or pillow is flexible, this will still create a small mound for him to crawl up and down.

26. Side to Side on the Ball

Starting Position: Sit your baby on the top of a large inflatable exercise ball. Sit in front of your baby holding him securely in this seated position with both your hands on his upper legs or around his waist for the best stability. Your baby should be able to sit independently before you attempt this activity. We recommend that you have another person help stabilize the ball.

Motion: Gently roll the exercise ball from side to side and in small circles as you hold your baby securely in a sitting position facing you. You should not move the ball more than about 6 inches in any direction. The objective is to move your seated baby's hips out from beneath his shoulders while keeping his bottom on the ball so your baby learns to maintain his balance by moving his upper body and hips as needed to compensate.

Make sure you move the ball very slowly and only a few inches at first. As you baby improves, you can move the ball in more directions and slightly farther.

Safety Tip: Your baby's sitting position on this activity is naturally unstable and it will become more so as you shift the ball beneath him. If you have any concerns about your baby's ability to do this activity or your ability to keep him stable on the exercise ball, then ask your spouse or a friend to help you keep your baby stable or try another activity. Always make sure you are in a good position to stabilize him if he should lose his balance and begin to fall off the ball. Make sure you are a safe distance from any furniture or objects that may hurt if you bump into them.

Muscles: This motion will require your baby to use various muscles throughout his hips, *abdomen* and back to maintain balance and his seated position.

You can make this activity more fun by:

A. Having another person offer toys to your baby from one side of the ball. Have your baby reach for the toy and pass it back to you or the other person.
B. Having your baby take a small basketball and toss it into a small net on one side of the ball.

27. Back Bend on the Ball

<u>Starting Position</u>: Sit your baby on the top of a large inflatable exercise ball. Sit in front of your baby holding him securely in this seated position with both your hands on his upper legs or around his waist for the best stability. Your baby should be able to sit independently before you attempt this activity. We recommend that you have another person help stabilize the ball.

<u>Motion</u>: Encourage and assist your baby to *slowly* lower himself backwards until he is lying with his back on the ball. As he lowers himself backwards, you can slowly roll the ball forward to prevent him from feeling like he is falling backwards into thin air. As you roll the ball forward, his hips will slide forward on the part off the ball rolling down and the part of the ball behind him will be rolling up to support his back. Assist him to use his abdominal muscles to return to sitting on top of the ball. Have him repeat this several times.

It will probably take some time until your baby is comfortable going backwards. He will also need some assistance returning to sitting upright.

As your baby's *abdominal* muscles strengthen, you may not have to roll the ball quite as much to assist with your baby's motion.

<u>Safety Tip</u>: In addition to the other safety tips included on other exercise ball activities, be aware of your baby's flexibility when attempting this activity because your baby will need to stretch his stomach muscles and ribcage and arch his back. You should have a larger exercise ball that is well inflated. The larger the exercise ball, the less he will need to arch his back and stretch his stomach.

<u>Muscles</u>: This motion focuses on the *abdominal* muscles.

You can make this activity more fun by:

    A. Having another person sit behind your baby. Give him a toy to hold as he lies backwards and tell him to give the toy to the person behind him when he is on his back. The person behind him can take the toy and give him another one which he can hold as he sits up.
    B. Playing "Peek-a-boo" to encourage him to lean back and sit up.

28. Wheel Barrow

<u>Starting Position</u>: Have your baby get in a four point crawling position up on his hands and knees. You should be kneeling at your baby's side as he crawls.

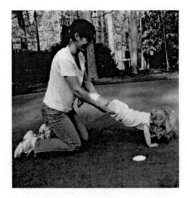

<u>Motion</u>: As your baby is crawling on his hands and knees, reach down with your hands and scoop up his lower body slightly off the floor, supporting most of his weight at the hips. Encourage him to continue to crawl using his arms and hands while you hold his lower body slightly up off the floor and walk on your knees to keep pace with his crawling.

Let him set the pace and do the crawling with his hands. If he is not able to keep walking on his hands as you support his lower body, try to just hold him in this position with his legs off the ground as he supports his weight on his arms. Lower his legs to the ground after a few seconds. After he becomes comfortable with the static position, try encouraging him to take a few steps with his hands and work your way up to more steps.

<u>Safety Tip</u>: This is a somewhat awkward and difficult move at first, and it will likely take some practice before your baby can take more than a few steps with his hands. Be careful to help your baby keep his balance and do not push him forward too fast. This could cause him to trip over his hands and fall on his face. It is best not to do this activity on a hard or rough surface.

<u>Muscles</u>: This motion improves strength and coordination in the arms, shoulders and back.

You can make this activity more fun by:

A. Placing a toy several feet away and having him crawl to get it.
B. Cutting baby-size handprints out of cartoon themed contact paper and sticking them on the floor as a visual image for where the baby should put his hands as you move together.

Level 3 – Cruises along Furniture

The following activities are best suited for a baby who is able to cruise along furniture.

Remember to take your baby's age and his physical and cognitive development into consideration when selecting toys to use during these activities. To be sure these activities are appropriate for your baby at this stage in his development, check with your *pediatrician* or *physical therapist* first.

29. Slide

<u>Starting Position</u>: Go to a local playground that has a small toddler slide that is relatively low to the ground and not too steep. See our web site's toy and product page for examples and recommendations if you want to purchase a playground cube for your baby. Sit your baby at the top of the slide with his legs in front of him.

<u>Motion</u>: Hold on to your baby and help him slide down the slide. When he gets to the bottom have him sit at the base of the slide and stand from this seated position. Try to make sure his knees and feet are pointed forward.

Then have him turn around and try to crawl back up the slide as you

hold and assist him. This will provide an incline for resistance and will be more difficult than crawling on a flat surface. If the incline is steep you will need to support more of his weight for him to climb up, so pay attention to how much assistance your baby needs. If it is too difficult for your baby to crawl up the slide, try crawling up a grassy hill instead. Try going up and down the slide several times.

<u>Safety Tip</u>: Supervise your baby closely and hold on to him to make sure he does not fall off the slide. Make sure the slide is low enough so that you can stand on the ground and hold your baby while at the top of the slide. Hold your baby as he slides down so that he does not fall forward or backward. It may take some time for him to get the hang of balancing himself. Make sure that there is not another child who wants to come down the slide as your baby is going up.

<u>Muscles</u>: As your baby goes down the slide he uses his *core* to stabilize himself. When he crawls back up the slide he must use his arm and leg muscles.

You can make this activity more fun by:

A. Rolling a car or pull toy down the slide so your baby can chase it down the slide.
B. Placing a toy at the top of the slide so that your baby must go "save" the toy in the tower.

30. Playing in a High Kneeling Position

<u>Starting Position</u>: Place your baby on his hands and knees. Help him to push off the floor with his hands and lift his upper body straight up so that his back is straight and he is bearing his weight on his knees. His bottom should not be resting on his heels and he should not be bent at the waist or arching his back.

<u>Motion</u>: Have your baby hold this position while playing. You can have him balance by holding on to a table or wall at first until he is able to hold this position independently. You can also elevate an adjustable aerobic step to a higher setting to encourage your baby to get into a high kneeling position to play with toys you place on the step. As he is playing, help him maintain good posture with his back straight. As your baby is playing throughout the day, try to incorporate this position.

After your baby is familiar with standing and playing on his knees, encourage him to try and walk on his knees. You will have to help support him at first by letting him hold your hand or by having him hold on to a push toy. Some babies will knee walk before they walk on their feet. Knee walking gives your baby a wider base of support and keeps him lower to the ground so it is easier to balance and not as scary for him. As he walks on his knees his shins and tops of his feet should be on the floor and his back should remain straight. Sometimes it helps to demonstrate for your baby first to show him what to do.

Our daughter loves to play with a refrigerator magnet set where you match the front and back of half of farm animals. When you place animal magnets in position, the toy sings a song. See our web site for this toy and other suggestions.

<u>Safety Tip</u>: Make sure that if your baby is leaning against a piece of furniture as he is kneeling that the furniture will not slide or tip under his weight.

<u>Muscles</u>: This activity strengthens the *abdomen*, lower back, hips, and legs. It also helps develop balance.

You can make this activity more fun by:

A. Placing toys in a basket with high sides so he must get into high kneeling position to get the toys out. Make sure the basket is sturdy and will not fall over.
B. Placing a piece of paper or a magnetic dry erase board on the refrigerator for him to draw on. You can raise the magnets or paper higher on the fridge so he transitions from kneeling to standing to continue playing in a standing position.
C. Having your child kneel in front of a play kitchen and take things in and out of the oven or fridge.
D. Having your baby play with age appropriate magnets on the refrigerator. Place the magnets at an appropriate height for him to kneel in front of.

31. Dress Up

<u>Starting Position</u>: Sit on the floor and have your baby stand facing you with his hands on your shoulders for support. Have him stand up as straight as possible with his feet shoulder width apart.

<u>Motion</u>: Help your baby get dressed as he stands in front of you. Have him let go with one hand at a time as you put each arm into his sleeves. Then have him lift each foot to put on pants. You can have him hold each foot in the air one at a time to put on his socks and shoes. If this is too difficult for him, try having him sit on a low stool and lift each foot off the ground as you put on his socks and shoes. Take your time as you do this so he lifts his leg and holds it in the air. As your baby is able to assist more, have him let go of one of your shoulders and squat down to grab the waistband of his pants to help pull them up. You can also do this activity at bath time to help your baby get undressed. Let him do as much as he can. This activity will also help develop his fine motor skills. Even if he must sit down to dress and undress, this is still good practice. This is also a great way to help your baby learn to identify body parts.

<u>Safety Tip</u>: Hold on to your baby as you do this. Make sure you are a safe distance from any objects that your baby may fall on.

<u>Muscles</u>: This activity strengthens the legs and works on your baby's balance and coordination.

You can make this activity more fun by:

    A. Singing the "Hokey Pokey" as you have him put his arms and legs in his clothes and shake them all about!
    B. Playing "Simon Says". Simon says put your left foot in the pants leg.

32. Ring Around the Table

<u>Starting Position</u>: Have your baby stand facing the coffee table holding on to it with both hands. Make sure his feet are flat on the floor and about shoulder width apart, and he is stable. His feet should be pointing forward toward the table.

<u>Motion</u>: Set up "toy stations" around the table so your baby can cruise around the table and play as he goes. The more interesting the toys, the more likely he will try to stand and cruise as long as possible. As he side steps around the table, make sure that his feet and knees are aligned. Make sure he is holding his upper body straight and not dragging either of his feet. Try to make him walk in both directions around the table. When he stops at a station, have him lift one foot up and place it on a low stool or phone book so that he bears more weight on the straight leg. If one of his legs seems to be weaker than the other, this is a good way to encourage him to stand on and develop the weaker leg.

<u>Safety Tip</u>: Make sure that whatever table you use it is sturdy enough not to tip under your baby's weight. It can also help to use table edge guards to soften some of the inevitable bumps that come along with learning to walk.

<u>Muscles</u>: This activity concentrates on the leg muscles. It helps develop balance and coordination. Depending on the stations you set up it can also help develop his *fine motor skills.*

You can make this activity more fun by:

A. Placing cereal or snacks around the table so that he cruises around the table picking up the snacks and eating as he goes. Make sure he chews and swallows before moving on.
B. Having him push a toy car around the top of the table.
C. Having your baby play at a music table or activity table.

We found a great activity table that adapts to your baby's development. When he is able to sit up independently you can put him in a seat on wheels attached to the round table so he can use his legs to push himself around the table. When he is able to stand and cruise you can remove the seat and it is at a perfect cruising height. The table is circular with different activities like a piano and an etch-a-sketch. This is better than the traditional exer-saucers where your baby remains stationary in the middle of the table. Lynn has played with this since she was 5 months old and has yet to tire of it. Check out on the toys and product page of our web site for this activity table and other similar toys that can encourage your baby to stand, cruise and play.

33. Parallel Walk

<u>Starting Position</u>: Have your baby stand between a coffee table and the sofa placing one hand on the table and the other hand on the sofa. You may need to push the table closer to the sofa so that he can hold both at the same time and still feel comfortable. Make sure he is standing up straight with his feet about shoulder width apart and pointing forward along the line between the sofa and table.

<u>Motion</u>: Have your baby walk forward in the space between the sofa and the table. Make sure he walks with his body facing forward instead of side stepping along either piece of furniture. This will get him familiar with the motion of walking forward with nothing in front of him while still providing him with the extra support he needs to remain standing. This motion also allows him to walk without your assistance to help develop confidence.

Try a variation of this motion by having him stand holding the edge of the coffee table that faces the open room (rather than the edge facing the sofa). Have him put one hand on the coffee table for support and you can hold his other hand as you walk on your knees beside him.

<u>Safety Tip</u>: Make sure your table is sturdy enough not to tip under your baby's weight. You can also put table edge guards on the table for added protection in case he stumbles.

<u>Muscles</u>: This activity develops the leg muscles while improving balance, coordination and confidence.

You can make this activity more fun by:

    A. Rolling a pull toy or car in front of him to chase.
    B. Placing his favorite toy at the other end of the table for him to walk to and play with.

34. Squat

<u>Starting Position</u>: Have your baby stand holding a wall or a piece of furniture for support. His feet should be about shoulder width apart and his feet facing forward.

<u>Motion</u>: Place a toy on the floor next to his feet. Encourage him to squat to reach the toy. You may need to assist him until he builds enough strength to do this independently. Help him control his body and use his legs to lower himself. Do not let him simply drop to the floor. He should come to a stop in a mid-level squatting position with his knees bent at a 90 degree angle and aligned above his feet. The objective is to hold this mid-level squat for a few seconds before returning to standing to focus the emphasis on the target leg muscles. Keep his knees and feet pointing forward. One hand can remain on the wall or furniture or he can hold your hand for support while he squats to pick up the toy with his other hand.

<u>Safety Tip</u>: If your baby starts by holding a piece of furniture, make sure the furniture is sturdy enough not to tip under your baby's weight.

<u>Muscles</u>: This activity strengthens the legs and improves balance.

You can make this activity more fun by:

    A. Having your baby lean onto the refrigerator for support and pick up age appropriate magnets from the floor and place them on the fridge. (Do not allow your baby to hang on the refrigerator door. Use caution to prevent any tipping.)
    B. Having him pick up play dishes from the floor and place them in the play kitchen sink. Make sure your baby does not place all his weight on the kitchen and cause it to tip over.
    C. Picking up stickers from the floor and placing them on a piece of paper on the wall. (Make sure your baby does not put the stickers in his mouth).

35. Start your engines – Ride-On Toy

<u>Starting Position</u>: Have your baby sit on a ride-on toy. Pick a riding toy that your child will enjoy whether it is a fire truck, a princess car or a classic tricycle. Some ride-on toys are also push toys. See the toys and products page of our web site for some suggestions. Make sure when he sits on the toy, his feet touch the ground with a slight bend in the knees – not a straight drop to the floor or a 90 degree bend at the knees but somewhere in between.

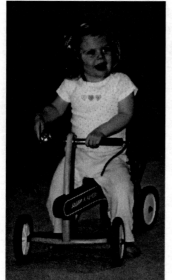

<u>Motion</u>: It may take him a few tries to figure out what to do with the ride-on toy, but be patient. Give him a few small pushes and pulls and show him what he must do with his feet to move forward. Work with him to use his feet to push off the ground and scoot the toy forward. Pay attention to his foot placement and help him place his feet pointing forward rather than pointing out to the sides to prevent extra pressure on his knees and ankles. Have him push himself with both feet at the same time or by alternating his feet. This is another fun way to get your baby learning to move independently.

<u>Safety Tip</u>: Make sure he has a clear path and will not run into anything that may fall over and hurt him. Also make sure he steers clear of any stairs.

Find a ride-on that is sturdy and that your baby will be able to steer. The toy should not force his feet to touch the floor more than his shoulder width apart. Wider, boxier riding toys that force a baby's legs to extend far out to their sides do not allow the baby to use the targeted muscle groups and can place extra pressure on hips, knees and ankles as he tries to push himself.

<u>Muscles</u>: This activity strengthens the *legs*, ankles and feet. It improves balance and coordination.

You can make this activity more fun by:

    A. Having your baby drive to the "grocery store" (your kitchen) to pick up some food.
    B. Having your baby drive his teddy bear to his "friend's house" to play.
    C. Having your baby park his car between furniture or toys. Provide a special prize for successful parallel parking.

36. Howdy Partner – Rocking Horse

<u>Starting Position</u>: Have your baby stand and hold onto a rocking horse. See the toys and products page on our web site for examples and recommendations for rocking horses.

<u>Motion</u>: Help your baby lift one leg and swing it over the horse while maintaining his balance and a firm grasp on the horse. Then have him push off the floor with the foot on the floor and slide his bottom onto the center of the rocking horse seat. Have him bend his elbows slightly as he holds on to the handles and use his body to make the horse rock back and forth. He should be sitting upright and may be bent forward slightly at the waist. You may have to assist a few times until he gets the idea of what to do with the rocking horse. Once he gets the hang of this, hopefully he will love it as much as Lynn.

<u>Safety tip</u>: Make sure you place the rocking horse away from all furniture and breakable items in case your baby gets a little rowdy. Look for a rocking horse that has a wide base of support to prevent it from tipping. Also look for one that is the appropriate distance from the ground so your baby will be able to get on and off without assistance.

<u>Muscles</u>: This activity strengthens the *core* muscles and arms during the rocking motion. This activity is also helpful for improving balance. Climbing up and down the rocking horse also strengthens the arm and leg muscles.

You can make this activity more fun by:

A. Making horse and galloping sounds while he rocks.
B. Turning on some country music to get into the cowboy mood.

Level 4 – Walks with Assistance

The following activities are best suited for a baby who is able to walk facing forward with the support of another person (as distinguished from cruising in a side stepping manner).

Remember to take your baby's age and his physical and cognitive development into consideration when selecting toys to use during these activities. To be sure these activities are appropriate for your baby at this stage in his development, check with your *pediatrician* or *physical therapist* first.

37. Circle the Wagons – Push Toys

<u>Starting Position</u>: Have your baby stand up behind a sturdy push toy (such as a wagon) holding on to the handle. He should be standing up straight with his feet about shoulder width apart and his knees and toes pointing forward. At first, he may lean forward as he begins to the push the toy, but in time and with your assistance, he should develop better posture and the ability to stand up straight behind the toy.

<u>Motion</u>: Have your baby push the toy forward and walk behind it. This is a great way to get him familiar with the feeling of walking and also allows him to do it independently. You should be prepared to slow him down if he builds up too much speed and risks losing control or falling. Be ready to help him steer when he first uses the toy. As he is walking, help him continue pointing his feet straight in the direction he is walking, and try to prevent him from leaning forward over the toy.

 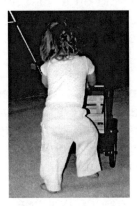

<u>Safety Tip</u>: Make sure to clear a path for your baby and the push toy so he will not knock anything down (e.g. side tables with lamps that could fall). Also never let him play near stairs. Look for a push toy that is sturdy and not so lightweight that it will topple when your baby tries to pull up on it or slide out from under him as he begins to push it.

Look for a push toy that has a wide base of support. We found a great walker wagon that your baby can fill up with his toys. When he is first using the push toy you can also put some phone books in the wagon to help weigh it down so it will not roll as fast. Our daughter also loved to sit in it so we could give her a ride. Visit the toys and products page of our web site for some examples and recommendations.

<u>Muscles</u>: This activity strengthens the legs and helps improve balance and coordination. It also helps build confidence.

You can make this activity more fun by:
    A. Giving your baby's favorite stuffed animal a ride on the push toy.
    B. Making car sounds as he pushes the push toy around.
    C. Setting up an obstacle course for him to navigate through.

38. Walk Up the Ball

<u>Starting Position</u>: Place a large exercise ball against a wall, preferably in a corner to keep the ball steady. Have another person help hold the ball steady. Stand facing the ball with your baby standing on the floor in front of you also facing the ball. Hold your baby from behind with your hands around his chest under his arms.

<u>Motion</u>: Encourage your baby to place his feet on the ball and "walk" up the exercise ball. Encourage him to press off the ball with his feet and step forward and up. As he takes steps with each foot, you should lift him higher so he progresses up the ball. His upper body should remain relatively vertical as he reaches forward and up with his feet for the next step. Once he has "walked" up to the top of the ball, you can hold on to him and have him bounce up and down with his feet on top of the ball. You can then sit him down on the ball and have him bounce or roll side to side as mentioned in previous activities. Take him off the ball and repeat this a few times.

<u>Safety tip</u>: Be very careful. It is very easy to lose control of the ball and have it roll away as your baby tries to take steps. If you can wedge the ball into corner or between some sturdy pieces of furniture, this can help control the ball.

Make sure not to place the ball near any objects that may fall and injure your baby if the ball rolls into them.

<u>Muscles</u>: This activity helps strengthen your baby's feet and ankles as he reaches and presses his feet against the ball. It also works the *quadriceps* as he lifts his legs up for the next steps. It should also help improve his balance and coordination.

You can make this activity more fun by:

    A. Having the person helping you balance the ball give your baby a high five at the top.
    B. Giving your baby a sticker to place on the shirt of the person helping you.
    C. Asking your baby, "How big are you?" when he gets to the top. Have him stretch tall and say, "So big!"

39. Backward Wall Stands

<u>Starting Position</u>: Have your baby sit on the floor about six inches in front of a wall with his back toward the wall.

<u>Motion</u>: Have him place his hands on the floor in front of him and get into a squatting or crouching position. Have him lean his bottom back slightly until it is up against the wall. Then have him straighten his legs while keeping his hands on the floor in front of him for balance. Have him maintain a slight bend in his knees. Then have him push off the floor with his hands and use his *back*, *hamstring* and *abdominal* muscles to come to standing leaning back against the wall. The wall provides him the extra support needed to stand up, and it teaches the general motion of standing even if your baby does not possess all the balance needed to stand completely on his own.

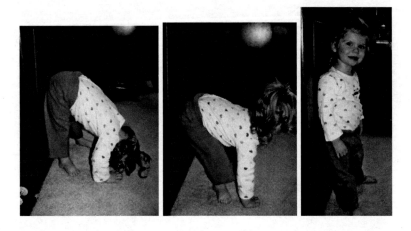

Help your baby sit down and stand up several times.

<u>Safety Tip</u>: Make sure you do this away from any furniture or objects on the floor that your baby may fall on. Also make sure he is not too far from the wall when he tries to stand up. If you try this up against a piece of furniture make sure it is sturdy enough not to tip or slide under his weight.

<u>Muscles</u>: This activity strengthens the *back, hamstrings* and *abdominal* muscles. It also improves balance. It gives your baby a sense of what it feels like to stand without pulling up on anything in front of him which is helpful for building confidence.

You can make this activity more fun by:

    A. Singing the "Itsy Bitsy Spider" or playing "Pat-a-Cake" when he comes to standing.
    B. Playing "Simon Says" while he is standing and have him point to different body parts.
    C. Singing "Head, Shoulders, Knees and Toes" as he stands up and sits down.
    D. Holding his favorite toy above him and encouraging him to stand and reach the toy.

40. Wall Postings

<u>Starting Position</u>: Have your baby stand facing the wall in a hallway or in a room with a lot of empty wall space. Have him lean slightly towards the wall to balance himself with his hands.

<u>Motion</u>: Encourage your baby to walk / cruise along the wall supporting himself with one or both hands on the wall. If he uses both hands on the wall, have him side step along the wall with his body and feet facing the wall. Try to make sure he does not drag or shuffle his feet as he walks but lifts and places his feet. When he has better balance and control you can work with him to use only one hand for support against the wall as he walks with his body parallel to the wall in a more normal forward walking motion.

<u>Muscles</u>: This activity strengthens the legs and improves balance, coordination and confidence.

You can make this activity more fun by:

    A. Placing 'sticky notes' along the wall and asking your baby to go get the notes off the wall. You can use this as an opportunity to teach shapes, colors, letters, numbers, etc. Color a few sticky notes with different colors and ask your baby to help you find the red, yellow or blue one. Draw shapes, letters or numbers and work with your baby to locate a particular one. Place the notes a few feet or yards away and have your baby walk to the proper note and return it to you for extra walking practice.

41. Follow in my footsteps

Starting Position: Go to a store and buy some non-permanent adhesive shelf liner with a fun theme. Trace an outline of a right and left foot slightly larger than your baby's foot on the shelf liner and cut out the footprints. Stick the footprints on your carpet in a walking pattern.

If you are worried about the adhesive on your carpet, test a small area first. We found the temporary adhesive helped prevent the footprints from sliding under our baby's feet.

Motion: Help your baby stand up behind the footprints and assist him based on his ability to walk on the footprints. Your baby could also use his push toy for support. Make sure that your baby has his back straight and is not leaning forward as he walks. The footprints allow your baby to visualize how and where to place his feet. We also found that by having the footprints there, our daughter wants to walk on them.

Muscles: This activity strengthens the leg muscles and improves balance, coordination and confidence.

You can make this activity more fun by:

   A. Having another person walk ahead and having your baby play 'follow the leader'.
   B. Rolling a pull toy in front of him to follow or having your baby's favorite toy to play with at the endpoint.

42. Baby Marionette

<u>Starting Position</u>: Have your baby stand with his feet about shoulder width apart with his feet pointing forward, and hold on to his hands.

<u>Motion</u>: Help your baby walk while he holds your hands. At first, it may help to kneel in front of him facing him and walk backwards on your knees as your baby walks forward. If you are in front of him, your assistance will not pull his arms back as you otherwise might if you were positioned behind him. It may also be easier on your back than leaning over to hold your baby's hand. As your baby walks, try not to let him lean forward or backwards. You can also have a person on both sides of your baby holding each of his hands as they help him walk. Be careful not to pull up on his arms or lift him up and swing him as this can dislocate his arms.

An alternative to holding his hands is to roll up a thin towel or sweatshirt and place it across your baby's chest and under his armpits with the loose ends coming out behind him and up from his shoulder blades. Hold and lift the two ends of the towel to help support part of your baby's weight (somewhat like a puppet, hence the name). This technique allows his arms to remain free in a more natural walking position, and you do not have to break your back bending over. You can purchase a product called Walker Wings ™ (a modified baby vest with cords and handles attached) that serves the same purpose. Check out the toys and products page of our web site for Walker Wings and other product suggestions.

When your baby is about ready to walk on his own and the only thing holding him back is confidence you can put a small object like a clothes pin or a small toy in each of your hands and have him hold on to the object. As your baby walks with more stability, you can let go of the object on your side, but he still feels like he is holding on to support. Only try this when your baby is no longer using you to help support his body weight.

<u>Safety Tip</u>: When attempting this activity, make sure you are on a soft surface like carpet or grass and that there is nothing close by for your baby to fall on if he stumbles.

<u>Muscles</u>: This activity strengthens the legs. It improves endurance, balance, coordination and confidence.

You can make this activity more fun by:

A. Setting up your baby's favorite toy several steps away and helping your baby walk to the toy.
B. Letting your baby or another person pull a doggie pull toy so you can walk the dog.
C. Walk from one room to the next, take a quick play break, and then walk to another room.

43. Walk Through Water

Starting Position: Have your baby stand in a shallow baby pool (12 – 15 inches deep) holding on to your hands for support.

Motion: Assist your baby to walk through the water in a similar manner to the "Baby Marionette" activity mentioned previously. The water will add resistance to his legs and body as he tries to walk. This resistance will force him to walk slowly and concentrate to keep his balance. Make sure he bends his knees and picks up his feet in proper walking form instead of just shuffling his feet along the bottom of the pool. Also try to keep him standing as upright as possible and try not to let him lean backwards or forwards as he walks. Remember to be careful as you are doing this.

Safety Tip: It is always a good idea to have a supervising adult or lifeguard trained in CPR and First Aid when playing in or near water.

Muscles: This is a great way to strengthen your baby's legs, and it can help him with his balance and coordination.

You can make this activity more fun by:

A. Walking to collect floating rubber ducks you have placed around the pool water or on the edges of the pool.
B. Seeing how much water he can splash up as he lifts his feet and legs to walk.
C. Walking a pool toy across to place in a bucket.

44. Walk the stairs

<u>Starting Position</u>: Have your baby stand at the base of the stairs. Hold him securely under his arms and around his chest. Have him stand with his feet about shoulder width apart with his toes pointing forward.

<u>Motion</u>: Support your baby as he lifts his right leg and places it on the first step in front of him. Encourage him to push through and straighten his right leg and come to a standing position. Make sure his right foot is pointed straight forward as much as possible (not pointing out to the side) and his knee is pointing in the same direction as his toes. He should lift his left leg up to the same step and place it next to his right foot so that both feet are together.

Have him repeat the motion starting with his left leg to stand up on the next step.

As your baby's walking ability improves, he will be able to alternate feet and place each foot on a separate step as he goes up the stairs. Make sure that as you support your baby he is standing upright and not leaning backwards or forwards.

<u>Safety Tip</u>: Be careful to hold your baby securely. Never allow your baby on the stairs unsupervised, and place safety gates at the top and bottom of the stairs to help deter your baby from accessing the stairs unsupervised. Your baby should be able to walk well with your assistance before trying this activity. Just try a few steps at first.

<u>Muscles</u>: This activity strengthens the legs. It also improves your baby's balance and coordination.

You can make this activity more fun by:

A. Walking up stairs to your front door or a neighbor's house and having your baby knock to see if anyone is home.
B. Having him walk up the stairs to take his bath.
C. Walking up a children's step stool with a couple of steps to reach the sink to brush his teeth.
D. Walking up the steps at a local playground to go down the slide.

45. Bear Crawl

<u>Starting Position</u>: Have your baby sit on the floor with his feet in front of him. Have him put his hands on the floor, palms down, and then get into a four point crawling position on his hands and knees. From this position, have him straighten his arms and legs so his body forms a pyramid shape with his bottom in the air.

<u>Motion</u>: Encourage your baby to take small "steps" with his hands and his feet, one at a time, from this position. It may take your baby some time to get the hang of this motion. You can demonstrate the motion to help him understand what to do. It is easy to tire quickly due to the intensity of this activity, so pay attention to your baby and make sure he takes breaks even if he seems to be enjoying himself. He can lower his bottom into a squatting position and then rise back up again.

Our daughter found this motion so fun, even after she could walk, she would still do this motion and make animal noises.

<u>Safety Tip</u>: Make sure there is a clear path ahead of your baby so he can move without running into objects. Your baby may get dizzy if he stays in this position too long, so make sure he does not lose his balance and fall.

<u>Muscles</u>: This activity works the arms, shoulders and chest muscles in the upper body and stretches the hamstring and calf muscles in the legs. It also improves balance and coordination.

You can make this activity more fun by:

A. Playing "Peek-a-boo" through his knees. Lynn loved to get into this position and look at us upside down and between her knees. She would walk away on all fours keeping an eye on us through her legs and giggling or making animal sounds as she went.
B. Pretending you are different animals and asking your baby what sound the animal makes. For example moo like a cow or bark like a dog.

Level 5 – Attempting to Stand and Walk Alone

The following activities are best suited for a baby who is attempting to stand alone and attempting to take a few steps alone.

Remember to take your baby's age and his physical and cognitive development into consideration when selecting toys to use during these activities. To be sure these activities are appropriate for your baby at this stage in his development, check with your *pediatrician* or *physical therapist* first.

46. Hand over Hand Standing

<u>Starting Position</u>: Have your baby sit on the floor with his feet in front of him. Have him put his hands on the floor, palms down, and then get into a four point crawling position on his hands and knees. From this position, have him straighten his arms and legs so his body forms a pyramid shape with his bottom in the air. Place several levels of stable and solid objects in front of him such as books or large blocks of increasing heights (e.g. 3, 8, 12 inches high).

<u>Motion</u>: If your baby is unable to stand on his own, this is a great activity to help teach him the way up. From the starting position, help your baby move one hand at a time from the floor to the lowest level object in front of him. Then help him move his hands to the next level object, and so on. As he walks, hand over hand, up the objects, he will have to adjust his balance as his center of gravity changes with each step. The objective is for your baby to straighten his arms from the highest level of objects in front of him and push himself to a standing position while you spot him for balance. Hopefully, you will enjoy the sight of that smile of accomplishment the first time your baby gets himself to standing "on his own" or at least without pulling up on you.

As your baby gets more comfortable with this activity, try removing the highest level, so he gets accustomed to less support from below and becomes more reliant on his own muscles, balance and ability to stand.

<u>Safety tip</u>: Make sure that the objects you place in front of your baby have a stable base and will not slide or slip out from under him when he places his weight on them.

<u>Muscles</u>: This activity focuses on the back and most of the leg muscles, particularly the *hamstrings*.

You can make this activity more fun by:

A. Singing the "Itsy Bitsy Spider" or playing "Pat-a-Cake" when he comes to standing.
B. Singing "Head, Shoulders, Knees and Toes" as he stands up and sits down.
C. Holding his favorite toy above him and encouraging him to stand and reach the toy.

47. Solo Standing

<u>Starting Position</u>: Sit with your baby on the floor in the middle of the room away from any furniture he could pull up on. Have your baby sit with his feet in front of him.

<u>Motion</u>: Have him put his hands on the floor, palms down, and then get into a four point crawling position on his hands and knees. From this position, have him straighten his arms and get into a crouched position. Help him to push off the floor with his hands and get into an upright standing position.

This is much easier said than done. Offer assistance as necessary to balance him, and as he becomes more familiar with the motion and the technique, offer less and less assistance until he can stand on his own. This is obviously a huge first component in helping your baby walk.

Once your baby gets to this standing position in the middle of the room, hold your baby around his waist until he appears steady and balanced. Subtly remove your hands from his waist, keeping them just an inch or so away, and see how long he can balance and stand on his own. You may not be able to remove your hands without him noticing and grabbing back on to you, particularly if he is not confident with standing. Try giving him a toy or ball to hold and distract him. One of the first times we tried this with Lynn, she stood for about 10 seconds simply because she was so focused on watching her mother in the other room, she just didn't realize she was standing unassisted. Building confidence is just as important as building muscles and balance.

If he still doesn't want you to let go of him, just reassure him that you will be right there to catch him if he starts to fall.

<u>Muscles</u>: The act of standing up works most of the body, but it particularly focuses on the back, the *core*, the *quadriceps* and the *hamstrings*. The solo-standing helps your baby improve balance and build confidence.

You can make this activity more fun by:

A. Demonstrating how to stand by singing and acting out "Head, Shoulders, Knees and Toes" and encouraging your child to imitate you.
B. Holding his favorite toy just above his reach from his seated position as extra motivation to stand and grab it.
C. Counting to track how long your baby stands on his own. Get louder and sound more excited as you get past certain numbers like 3, 5, 10, etc.

48. Get outside

<u>Starting Position</u>: If the weather is agreeable, go outside and play with your baby. Sometimes just changing the scenery is enough to make ordinary activities more fun and interesting for your baby. It will also give him more space to move around in without running in to anything.

<u>Motion</u>: Depending on your baby's ability, help him to walk around outside by holding his hands or using the techniques discussed in the Baby Marionette (activity # 42) or you can have your baby use his push toy for support. Lynn had a therapeutic walker on loan from our physical therapist, and Lynn loved to take it outside to walk and explore. Find some slight hills or inclines for your baby to walk up and down either in the grass or on pavement. The different terrains available outside can help your baby use different muscles to balance and stabilize his body. Walking through the grass and on an incline provides some great resistance. He must also use and flex different muscles to slow himself while walking on a decline. Walking in the grass may be more difficult, but the grass also provides a natural cushion for falls.

<u>Safety tip</u>: Stay close by until your baby becomes comfortable on these new surfaces. Falling on the driveway will hurt a lot more than on the grass, so make sure your baby has proper clothes to help guard against scraped knees. Be sure your baby's path is clear, try to remove large pinecones and sticks, and check for holes in the grass. If your baby is using a push toy or anything on wheels, make sure they do not pick up too much speed. And of course be smart about traffic and make sure your baby does not venture into the street.

<u>Muscles</u>: This activity strengthens the legs. It improves balance, coordination, and confidence.

You can make this activity more fun by:
- A. Walking to the end of the driveway to get the newspaper or check the mail. This was a daily activity for Lynn that she would not let us forget.
- B. Taking your doggie pull toy for a walk.
- C. Placing large plastic toys on the grass for your baby to pick up.
- D. Looking for birds in the trees and other animals outside.
- E. Walking to a friendly neighbor's house and knocking on the door to see if they are home.

49. Baby Steps

<u>Starting Position</u>: Have your baby pull up on a table, chair or other piece of furniture. Sit on the floor a few feet away just out of his reach. Encourage your baby to walk to you. Reach your hands out for your baby so that he feels confident that although you are sitting a couple feet away, your hands are right there to catch him if he stumbles.

<u>Motion</u>: Your baby should try to take just a couple steps to reach you. Even if it simply amounts to stumbling into your lap at first, that is a good start! He may hold his hands out to his sides for balance like a tightrope walker or in front of him as if bracing for an inevitable fall. He may squat low to the ground before pushing off. Any of this is okay. You just want him to make an effort to take a couple steps, but even if he does not, you still want him to start thinking about it and understand what you want him to do.

If he does stumble, help him stand again and encourage him to take a couple steps to reach you. Repeat this a couple times. Smile, laugh, and do not get frustrated. Remember, he is not going to get this right away, but we hope that he will eventually.

If he does take a couple steps, make sure he gets some congratulations, a great big hug or his favorite snack. Try to resist the temptation to move backwards and require more and more steps out of him. As we mentioned earlier in the book, this might backfire and damage his confidence and incentive to walk if he sees you constantly backing away just beyond his reach.

<u>Safety Tips</u>: Make sure his path is clear and you are a safe distance from any objects that may fall and injure him.

<u>Muscles</u>: This activity works all the major muscles in the legs, but this activity is mainly about confidence. Before Lynn stood on her own, she could do many activities with our assistance. Many people, our *pediatrician* and *physical therapist* included, said they thought Lynn could do a lot more than she knew or understood. She had the capability but not the confidence.

You can make this activity more fun by:

    A. Setting up a baby basketball net a couple feet away and encouraging your baby to take the 2 steps necessary to "slam dunk" the ball.
    B. Place his favorite "stand up" toy (e.g. a push toy or activity table) just a couple feet away and use that as his goal for walking.

50. Relay Race

Starting Position: Have your baby get to a standing position by either pulling up on some furniture or standing up solo from the floor. Have two other people stand or squat on the floor at positions 3 - 5 feet away and 8 - 10 feet away from your baby.

Motion: Encourage and call for your baby to take just a couple steps to reach the nearest person. Once he reaches the nearest person, make sure he receives lots of enthusiastic congratulations while he continues to stand. Then point him in the direction of the next person. If your baby is holding your hands, get him to release your hands and steady him until he starts to move towards the next person. Encourage him to walk to the next person in line – just a few steps away in the same direction. The first person can walk to the other side of the second person and repeat this exchange so that a few exchanges will help your baby walk across a room with only intermittent assistance.

This activity helps teach your baby that he can get from one place to another by walking instead of crawling. Instead of your baby walking back and forth between two people and not actually "getting somewhere", people can shift positions as discussed so that your baby can walk across the room or from one room to another. The next step is creating more distance between the stopping points to build your baby's strength and confidence. Resist the temptation to add too much distance too quickly.

Safety Tips: Make sure that you are a safe distance from any objects that your baby may fall and injure himself on.

Muscles: Technically, this activity works all the major muscles in the legs, but this activity is also all about confidence and teaching your baby that he can get from one place to another by walking.

You can make this activity more fun by:

- A. Setting up different toy stations at various distances, so he can walk from one toy to another and perhaps walk to people in between the toy stations.
- B. Placing his favorite toy at the other end of the room as an incentive to walk to the other side of the room.

Conclusion

We hope you found this book helpful in some way. Our goal is for other parents to learn from our personal experiences, research efforts, successes and mistakes along our path to helping Lynn walk. We know firsthand how concerning it is to think your baby is not "on track" with walking or some other early developmental milestone. We encourage all parents struggling with these concerns to be proactive, talk with your *pediatrician* and take reasonable measures to determine whether you baby has any diagnosable conditions that may require special attention. Whether or not special attention, such as physical therapy, is recommended, always be sure to listen to your parental instincts about what is best for your baby.

Remember – do not rush your baby. Instead of setting deadlines, just try to set eventual goals and work toward those goals with patience and persistence.

As you and your baby work toward the goal of walking, we hope this book has provided some useful information and encouragement to help you advocate for your baby with a *pediatrician* and other specialists. We also hope this book has provided you with some good questions and ideas to discuss with your baby's doctor(s) to help you navigate some of the complex healthcare issues facing babies with developmental delays or disabilities.

As you work with your *pediatrician*, other medical specialists, and your family and friends to help your baby walk, remember there are other resources available to help you and your baby. The resources range from support groups for people dealing with similar situations to government resources offering services and financial assistance.
We also hope that in combination with proper medical diagnosis and treatment from your *pediatrician* and other medical specialists, the games and activities described in this book can provide you with many fun ways to personally help your baby develop the strength, balance, coordination, muscle control, and confidence needed to walk. We wish you and your baby the very best of luck.

Glossary

Adenoids – mass of tissue found behind the nose in the upper part of the throat (*Definition of Adenoids,* 1998).

Calf muscles – a pair of muscles at the back of the lower leg (Wikipedia contributors, 2009, April 29).

Cardiologist – a physician who specializes in treating heart disorders (*Definition of Cardiologist,* 1999).

Cerebral palsy – a non progressive motor skill disorder caused by abnormal development or damage to the brain (*Cerebral Palsy,* n.d.).

Co-pay – a payment determined by an insurance policy that is paid by the insured person each time a medical service is provided (Wikipedia contributors, 2009, April 23).

Core – the muscles in your back, abdomen and pelvis (Wikipedia contributors, 2009, May 6).

CT scan – (computed tomography) a diagnostic scan that uses x rays to create images of anatomy (Wikipedia contributors, 2009, May 7).

Deductible – a set amount determined by the insurance company that must be paid by the insured before any expenses will be covered (Wikipedia contributors, 2009, April 26).

Dermatologist – a doctor who specializes in the diagnosis and treatment of skin disorders (*Definition of Dermatologist,* 1998).

Down syndrome – a chromosome abnormality, usually due to an extra copy of the twenty-first chromosome (*Hypotonia,* n.d.).

DAFO (Dynamic Ankle Foot Orthosis) – a plastic ankle, foot, or lower leg brace that is custom made to mold to an individual's foot and provide support (Haines, n.d.).

Early Intervention Program – special services for infants and toddlers who have a developmental delay or who are at risk for a developmental delay (National Dissemination Center for Children with Disabilities, 1994).

ENT (Ear, Nose and Throat Doctor) – (also known as otolaryngologist) doctor that specializes in disorders and treatment of the head and neck specifically the ears, nose, and throat (*Definition of ENT Physician,* 2003).

Explanation of benefits – a written statement from an insurance company after a claim has been made by a provider outlining what services and charges are covered or not covered under the insured's plan and who is responsible for payment (Mosby's Medical Dictionary, 2009).

Fine motor skills – fine motor skills generally refer to the small movements of the hands, wrists, fingers, feet, toes, lips, and tongue (*Hypotonia,* n.d.).

Flexible spending account – an account that employees can contribute pretax dollars into to use on qualifying medical expenses and child care. This money is not subject to payroll taxes (Wikipedia contributors, 2009, March 28).

Gastroenterologist – a doctor who specializes in diagnosing and treating diseases of the gastrointestinal tract (*Definition of Gastroenterologist,* 2004).

Gastroesophageal reflux – backward flow of contents from the stomach into the esophagus (*Sudden Infant Death,* n.d.).

Geneticist – a scientist who studies the relationship between genes and the traits that are observed in living things (*Definition of geneticist*, n.d.).

Gluteal muscles – the three large muscles that make up the buttock (*Gluteal Muscle,* n.d.).

Gross motor skills – the abilities required in order to control the large muscles of the body for walking, running, sitting, crawling, and other activities (*Hypotonia,* n.d.).

Group health insurance – a single policy under which individuals in a group, such as employees, and their dependents are covered (*Group Life or Group*, n.d.).

Hamstrings – the three muscles at the back of the thigh (*Hamstring*, 2009).

Hip Flexors – a group of skeletal muscles that act to pull the knee upward (Wikipedia contributors, 2009, March 24).

Hypothyroidism – a disorder that results from decreased thyroid hormone production (*Hypotonia,* n.d.).

Hypotonia – decreased muscle tone (*Hypotonia,* n.d.).

Individual private health insurance – health insurance purchased by an individual for himself and/or his family that is not provided by the government and is not in association with an employer (*Private Insurance Plans*, n.d.).

Karyotype – a test to identify any genetic abnormalities in a person's chromosomes that may cause a problem with his development and body functions (Essig, 2007).

Marfan Syndrome – an inherited disorder of connective tissue (tissue that adds strength to the body's structures), affecting the skeletal system, cardiovascular system, eyes, and skin (*Hypotonia,* n.d.).

Medicaid – a government program that is administered by the states to assist financially needy people to cover medical costs (*Medicaid,* n.d.).

MRI (Magnetic Resonance Imaging) – a radiology technique that uses magnetism, radio waves, and a computer to create pictures of body structures (Shiel, n.d.).

Multiple sclerosis – an autoimmune disease of the central nervous system that causes progressive paralysis (*Movement Disorders,* n.d.).

Muscle memory – the muscles ability to remember how to perform motor skills (Wikipedia contributors, 2009, May 1).

Muscular dystrophy - a group of disorders characterized by progressive muscle weakness and loss of muscle tissue (*Hypotonia,* n.d.).

Myasthenia gravis - a neuromuscular disorder characterized by variable weakness of voluntary muscles, which often improves with rest and worsens with activity. The condition is caused by an abnormal immune response (*Hypotonia,* n.d.).

Neurologist – a doctor who specializes in the disorders and treatment of the nervous system which includes the brain, spinal cord, and peripheral nerves (*Definition of Neurologist,* 1998).

Oblique abdominal muscles – the largest and outermost abdominal muscle on the front of the abdomen (Wikipedia contributors, 2009, May 2).

Occupational therapy – therapy that improves or recovers a person's ability to perform activities of daily living. It may allow a person to compensate for a permanent disability. The goal is to allow a person to function as independently as possible (Wikipedia contributors, 2009, March 30).

Orthopedist – a doctor specializing in the treatment of the musculoskeletal system (*Movement Disorders,* ,n.d.).

Orthotics – a support, brace, or splint used to support, align, or correct movable parts of the body (*Definition of Orthotic,* 2004).

Orthotist – a healthcare professional who specializes in making and fitting orthopedic appliances (Mosby's Medical Dictionary, 2009).

Pediatrician – a doctor who specializes in the care and treatment of infants and children (Mosby's Medical Dictionary, 2009).

Pediatric surgeon – a doctor who specializes in the treatment of children with conditions that can be surgically corrected (*Pediatric Surgery*, n.d.).

Physical therapist – a licensed medical professional who evaluates and treats physical impairments using exercises to improve function and independence (Mosby's Medical Dictionary, 2009).

Prader-Willi syndrome – a congenital disease characterized by obesity, severe *hypotonia*, and decreased mental capacity (*Hypotonia,* n.d.).

Pre-existing condition – any health condition that you already have when enrolling in a health insurance plan (Montgomery, 2008).

Premium – the amount of money paid each month to a health insurance company for coverage.

Pulmonologist – a doctor who specializes in the treatment of diseases of the respiratory tract (*What is a Pulmonologist*, n.d.).

Quadriceps – a large muscle group on the front of the thigh (Wikipedia contributors, 2009, April 24).

Radiologist – a doctor who specializes in imaging technology to treat and diagnose diseases (Wikipedia Contributors, 2009, May 4).

Spinal muscular atrophy type 1 (Werdnig-Hoffman): a group of inherited diseases causing progressive muscle degeneration and weakness, eventually leading to death (*Hypotonia,* n.d.).

Tay-Sachs disease – a genetic disorder found predominantly in Ashkenazi Jewish families results in early death (*Hypotonia,* n.d.).

Walking skills – a term we have used throughout the book to refer collectively to the strength, stamina, balance, coordination, muscle control, and confidence needed to walk.

References

About family voices. (n.d.). Retrieved April 27, 2009, from Family Voices Web site: http://www.familyvoices.org/info/about.php

Annual appropriations and number of children served under Part C of IDEA federal fiscal years 1987-2009. (n.d.). Retrieved April 27, 2009, from The National Early Childhood Technical Assistance Center Web site: http://www.nectac.org/partc/ partcdata.asp

Bradford, S. L. (2008, January 7). Buying private health insurance. *SmartMoney*. Retrieved February 23, 2009, from http://www.smartmoney.com/spending/deals/ buying-private-health-insurance-14819/

Cerebral palsy. (n.d.). Retrieved May 5, 2009, from Encyclopedia of children's health: Infancy through adolescence database: http://www.healthofchildren.com/C/ Cerebral-Palsy.html

COBRA continuation coverage assistance under the American Recovery and Reinvestment Act. (n.d.). Retrieved April 27, 2009, from U.S. Department of Labor Web site: http://www.dol.gov/ebsa/COBRA.html

Continuation of health coverage - COBRA. (n.d.). Retrieved April 27, 2009, from U.S. Department of Labor Web site: http://www.dol.gov/dol/topic/health-plans/ cobra.htm

Definition of adenoids. (1998, March 26). Retrieved May 8, 2009, from MedicineNet Web site: http://www.medterms.com/script/main/art.asp?articlekey=2147

Definition of cardiologist. (1999, November 14). Retrieved May 8, 2009, from MedicineNet Web site: http://www.medterms.com/script/main/ art.asp?articlekey=11097

Definition of dermatologist. (1998, March 26). Retrieved May 8, 2009, from MedicineNet Web site: http://www.medterms.com/script/main/art.asp?articlekey=2953

Definition of ENT physician. (2003, November 13). Retrieved May 8, 2009, from MedicineNet Web site: http://www.medterms.com/script/main/ art.asp?articlekey=25244

Definition of gastroenterologist. (2004, March 9). Retrieved May 7, 2009, from MedicineNet Web site: http://www.medterms.com/script/main/ art.asp?articlekey=3553

Definition of geneticist. (n.d.). Retrieved November 18, 2009, from EverythingBio Web site: http://www.everythingbio.com/glos/definition.php?word=geneticist

Definition of neurologist. (1998, March 26). Retrieved May 6, 2009, from MedicineNet Web site: http://www.medterms.com/script/main/art.asp?articlekey=4553

Definition of Orthotic. (2004, October 30). Retrieved May 6, 2009, from MedicineNet Web site: http://www.medterms.com/script/main/art.asp?articlekey=40206

Diseases and conditions. (n.d.). Retrieved February 22, 2009, from The Johns Hopkins Hypotonia Center Web site: http://www.hopkinsmedicine.org/geneticmedicine/ Clinical_Resources/Hypotonia/index.html

Early intervention program for infants and toddlers with disabilities (Part C of IDEA). (n.d.). Retrieved April 27, 2009, from The National Early Childhood Technical Assistance Center Web site: http://www.nectac.org/partc/partc.asp

Essig, M. G. (2007, April 26). *Karyotype test.* Retrieved May 6, 2009, from Web MD Web site: http://www.webmd.com/baby/karyotype-test

Expenditures on children by families, 2007 [Miscellaneous Publication Number 1528-2007]. (n.d.). Retrieved February 22, 2009, from U.S. Department of Agriculture Center for Nutrition Policy and Promotion Web site: http://www.cnpp.usda.gov/ Publications/CRC/crc2007.pdf

Gluteal muscle. (n.d.). Retrieved May 7, 2009, from The Free Dictionary Web site: http://www.thefreedictionary.com/gluteal+muscle

Group life or group health insurance. (n.d.). Retrieved May 7, 2009, from Nolo Web site: http://www.nolo.com/definition.cfm/Term/17EF3D57-E263-4E8A-B0B242103CB418E9/alpha/G/

Haines, W. A. (n.d.). *The Cascade Dynamic Ankle Foot Orthosis (DAFO) .* Retrieved May 8, 2009, from Maxcare Bionics Web site: http://maxcarebionics.com/pdfs/ articles/orthotic/lower_limb/cascade_dafo_article_052206.pdf

Hamstring. (2009). Retrieved May 7, 2009, from Merriam-Webster Online Dictionary Web site: http://www.merriam-webster.com/dictionary/hamstring

Himmelstein, D. U., Warren, E., Thorne, D., & Woolhandler, S. (2005, February 5). MarketWatch: Illness and injury as contributors to bankruptcy. *Health affairs: The policy journal of the health sphere.* Retrieved February 22, 2009. doi:10.1377/ hlthaff.w5.63

Hypotonia. (n.d.). Retrieved February 20, 2009, from Encylopedia of children's health: Infancy through adolescence database: http://www.healthofchildren.com/G-H/ Hypotonia.html

Medicaid. (n.d.). Retrieved May 6, 2009, from Nolo Web site: http://www.nolo.com/ definition.cfm/Term/67ED8716-B0D4-4C9D-A81701873DB0502C/alpha/M/

Milestone charts: What you can expect from birth to age 3. (2006, September).
Retrieved February 20, 2009, from Baby Center Web site:
http://www.babycenter.com/milestone-charts-birth-to-age-3

Montgomery, K. (2008, June 5). *Pre-existing condition.* Retrieved May 6, 2009, from
http://healthinsurance.about.com/od/glossary/g/preex1.htm

Mosby's Medical Dictionary. (2008). *Explanation of Benefits.* Retrieved June 9, 2009,
from The Free Dictionary Web site:
http://medicaldictionary.thefreedictionary.com/Explanation+Of+Benefits

Mosby's Medical Dictionary. (2009). *Orthotist.* Retrieved May 6, 2009, from The Free
Dictionary Web site: http://medical-dictionary.thefreedictionary.com/orthotist

Mosby's Medical Dictionary. (2009). *Pediatrician.* Retrieved May 6, 2009, from The Free
Dictionary Web site: http://medical-dictionary.thefreedictionary.com/pediatrician

Mosby 's Medical Dictionary. (2009). *Physical therapist.* Retrieved May 6, 2009, from
The Free Dictionary Web site: http://medical-dictionary.thefreedictionary.com/
physical+therapist

Movement Disorders. (n.d.). Retrieved May 6, 2009, from Encyclopedia of Children's
Health: Infancy through Adolescence Web site: http://www.healthofchildren.com/
M/Movement-Disorders.html

National Coalition on Health Care. (2009). *Health insurance coverage.* Retrieved
February 22, 2009, from http://www.nchc.org/facts/coverage.shtml

National Dissemination Center for Children with Disabilities. (n.d.). *Overview of early
intervention.* Retrieved February 20, 2009, from http://www.nichcy.org/babies/
overview/Pages/default.aspx

National Dissemination Center for Children with Disabilities. (1994, August). *A parent's
guide: Finding help for young children with disabilities (birth-5)* (2nd Edition ed.)
[Brochure]. Retrieved May 7, 2009, from http://www.nichcy.org/
InformationResources/Documents/NICHCY%20PUBS/pa2.pdf

Pediatric surgery. (n.d.). Retrieved May 6, 2009, from Encyclopedia of Surgery: A Guide
for Patients and Caregivers Web site: http://www.surgeryencyclopedia.com/Pa-
St/Pediatric-Surgery.html

Private insurance plans. (n.d.). Retrieved May 6, 2009, from Encyclopedia of Surgery: A
Guide for Patients and Caregivers Web site:
http://www.surgeryencyclopedia.com/Pa-St/Private-Insurance-Plans.html

17 surprising facts about birth in the United States. (2008, January). Retrieved April 23,
2009, from Baby Center Web site: http://www.babycenter.com/0_17-surprising-
facts-about-birth-in-the-united-states_1372273.bc

Shelov, S. P., Hannemann, R. E., & Trubo, R. (2004). *The American Academy of Pediatrics: The complete and authoritative guide: Caring for your baby and young child: Birth to age 5* (P. F. Agran, T. R. Altmann, S. S. Baker, W. L. Coleman, P. H. Dworkin, H. C. Meissner, et al., Eds., 4th ed.). United States of America: Bantam. (Original work published 1991)

Shiel, W. C., Jr. (n.d.). *Magnetic resonance imaging.* Retrieved May 6, 2009, from http://www.medicinenet.com/mri_scan/article.htm

Sudden infant death syndrome. (n.d.). Retrieved May 7, 2009, from Encyclopedia of Children's Health: Infancy through Adolescence Web site: http://www.healthofchildren.com/S/Sudden-Infant-Death-Syndrome.html

What docs should know about the Part C early intervention program. (n.d.). Retrieved February 20, 2009, from Docs for Tots Web site: http://www.docsfortots.org/resources/talkingPoints/documents/PartCEarlyIntervention.pdf

What is a pulmonologist? (n.d.). Retrieved May 6, 2009, from Pulmonology Channel Web site: http://www.pulmonologychannel.com/pulmonologist.shtml

What is parent to parent? (n.d.). Retrieved April 27, 2009, from Parent to Parent USA Web site: http://www.p2pusa.org/

Wikipedia contributors. (2009, March 24). *Hip flexors.* Retrieved May 6, 2009, from Wikipedia, The Free Encyclopedia Web site: http://en.wikipedia.org/wiki/Hip_flexor

Wikipedia contributors. (2009, March 28). *Flexible spending account.* Retrieved May 7, 2009, from Wikipedia, The Free Encyclopedia Web site: http://en.wikipedia.org/wiki/Flexible_spending_account

Wikipedia contributors. (2009, March 30). *Occupational therapist.* Retrieved May 6, 2009, from Wikipedia, The Free Encyclopedia Web site: http://en.wikipedia.org/wiki/Occupational_Therapist

Wikipedia contributors. (2009, April 24). *Quadriceps femoris muscle.* Retrieved May 6, 2009, from Wikipedia, The Free Encyclopedia Web site: http://en.wikipedia.org/wiki/Quadriceps

Wikipedia contributors. (2009, May 1). *Muscle memory.* Retrieved May 6, 2009, from Wikipedia, The Free Encyclopedia Web site: http://en.wikipedia.org/wiki/Muscle_memory

Wikipedia contributors. (2009, May 2). *Abdominal external oblique muscle.* Retrieved May 6, 2009, from Wikipedia, The Free Encyclopedia Web site: http://en.wikipedia.org/wiki/Abdominal_external_oblique_muscle

Wikipedia contributors. (2009, May 4). *Radiology*. Retrieved May 6, 2009, from Wikipedia, The Free Encyclopedia Web site: http://en.wikipedia.org/wiki/Radiologist

Wikipedia contributors. (2009, April 23). *Copayment*. Retrieved May 8, 2009, from Wikipedia, The Free Encyclopedia Web site: http://en.wikipedia.org/wiki/Copay

Wikipedia contributors. (2009, April 26). *Deductible*. Retrieved May 8, 2009, from Wikipedia, The Free Encyclopedia Web site: http://en.wikipedia.org/wiki/Deductible

Wikipedia contributors. (2009, April 29). *Calf muscle*. Retrieved May 8, 2009, from Wikipedia, The Free Encyclopedia Web site: http://en.wikipedia.org/wiki/Calf_muscle

Wikipedia contributors. (2009, May 6). *Core (anatomy)*. Retrieved May 8, 2009, from Wikipedia, The Free Encyclopedia Web site: http://en.wikipedia.org/wiki/Core_(anatomy)

Wikipedia contributors. (2009, May 7). *Computed tomography*. Retrieved May 8, 2009, from Wikipedia, The Free Encyclopedia Web site: http://en.wikipedia.org/wiki/Ct_scan

Wong, D. L., Hockenberry-Eaton, M., Wilson, D., Winkelstein, M. L., & Schwartz, P. (2001). Health promotion of the infant and family. In S. Schrefer, L. Wilson, M. Drone, & M. D. Hayden (Eds.), *Wong's essential's of pediatric nursing* (6th ed., pp. 331-383). St. Louis: Mosby. (Original work published 1982)

Wong, D. L., Hockenberry-Eaton, M., Wilson, D., Winkelstein, M. L., & Schwartz, P. (2001). Health promotion of the toddler and family. In S. Schrefer, L. Wilson, M. Drone, & M. D. Hayden (Eds.), *Wong's essential's of pediatric nursing* (6th ed., pp. 412-437). St. Louis: Mosby. (Original work published 1982)

Wright, P. W., & Wright, P. D. (n.d.). *Early intervention (Part C of IDEA)*. Retrieved February 20, 2009, from Wrightslaw Web site: http://www.wrightslaw.com/info/ei.index.htm

You are an advocate for your child with special health care needs! (n.d.). Retrieved February 20, 2009, from Family Voices Web site: http://www.familyvoices.org/pub/general/YouAreAnAdvocate.pdf

Lightning Source UK Ltd.
Milton Keynes UK
UKOW011826220812

197944UK00004B/11/P